I RETURNED AND SAW UNDER THE SUN

I
RETURNED
AND SAW
UNDER THE SUN

PADRE MARTÍNEZ OF TAOS

A Play

E. A. MARES

University of New Mexico Press

Albuquerque

Library of Congress Cataloging-in-Publication Data

Mares, E. A. 1938–
I returned and saw under the sun : Padre Martínez of Taos : a play
/ E. A. Mares. — 1st ed.
p.   cm.
Bibliography: p.
ISBN 0-8263-1128-8 : $22.50. ISBN 0-8263-1129-6 (pbk.) : $10.95
1. Martínez, Antonio José, 1793–1867—Drama. 2. Taos (N.M.)—
–History—Drama. 3. New Mexico—History—Drama. I. Title.
PS3563.A646812   1989
812'.54—dc 19   88-30842
CIP

For my parents,
Ernest G. and Rebecca Devine Mares

CONTENTS

I RETURNED AND SAW UNDER THE SUN

Padre Antonio José Martínez: Stage Center

A PERSONAL MEMOIR
AND HISTORIOGRAPHIC ESSAY

Many roads led to the writing of this play. Some of them were the simple paths of quiet reading and reflection that most writers take. Others involved extended research that took me to Spain in 1973, for example, on a Ford Foundation Travel and Study Grant to do archival work related to Padre Antonio José Martínez. Although much of the research was frustrating and seemingly led nowhere, I gradually came to realize that elements of the character, motivation, intelligence, and passion of Padre Martínez could best be approached through a judicious combination of historical documentation with the techniques of fiction. Specifically, the stage was an appropriate vehicle to capture a sense of the immediacy of Padre Martínez.

During the summer of 1982, the New Mexico Endowment for the Humanities (then known as the New Mexico Humanities Council), the state division of the National Endowment for the Humanities, sponsored a Chautauqua Program. Modeled on the nineteenth-century Chautauqua educational experiment, the program combined education in history with entertainment. Humanities scholars shared their historical knowledge by means of dramatizations of historically significant personalities that were performed in many communities throughout the state of New Mexico.

This Chautauqua Program was one path that led me back to Padre Antonio José Martínez of Taos. I had had earlier encounters with him. In the 1970s, Padre Martínez was an enigma to me. There was so much interest surrounding this priest and yet there was only a slim body of historical evidence documenting his life and times. The only popular portrayal of him, moreover, by Willa Cather in her curious hybrid novel, *Death Comes for the Archbishop,* was almost entirely negative. At the same time, there was no question that the historical and legendary Padre Martínez had become a significant folk hero for many *nuevomexicanos.*

Who was this priest from Taos? The bare bones of his biography indicate something of the complexity of his life. He was born in Abiquiu, New Mexico, in 1793 and died in Taos in 1867, at the age of seventy-four. His life thus spans the late stages of the disintegration of the Spanish Empire in the New World, the end of Spanish rule in Mexico, the establishment of an independent Republic of Mexico that remained sovereign in the Southwest (Mexico's northernmost province) from 1821 to 1846, and after that year, the first two decades of United States jurisdiction in New Mexico. He lived, then, under three distinct sovereignties: Spanish, Mexican, and American.

Antonio José Martínez attended a school in Abiquiu, possibly at a quite early age, and later he was trained as a

rancher and businessman to assist his father, Antonio Severino Martínez, in his extensive ranching and commercial
interests along the Camino Real, or the Chihuahua Trail,
which stretched north from central Mexico to that nation's
northern outposts in Santa Fe and Taos. The young Martínez married María de la Luz Martín. The marriage ended in
tragedy, however, for the young woman died during childbirth a year later. The child, a daughter named María de la
Luz in honor of her mother, was safely delivered but sur-
vived, nevertheless, only to age twelve.

Now a young widower, Antonio José Martínez turned his
attention to spiritual matters and in 1816 entered the Tridentine Monastery in Durango, Mexico, to study for the
priesthood. He was an excellent student even though the
tumultuous politics of the Mexican movement for independence from Spain undoubtedly offered many distractions.
He was ordained a priest and returned to New Mexico to
begin practicing his ministry in 1823.

After the death of his daughter in 1825, Padre Martínez
developed his many and varied interests and talents. He
opened a school in Taos for both boys and girls in 1833,
unusual as it was to educate both sexes at that time, and
also a "first" in the sense that this was the first major school
in New Mexico. In 1835, he purchased a printing press and
began to publish religious and educational materials. He
published a book on Spanish orthography that year, the first
book published in New Mexico.

He also renewed his interest in politics. He advocated a
humanitarian policy of treatment for the Indians of the
Southwest and he warned of the danger of extermination of

the buffalo. His recommendations on these matters were communicated to the President of Mexico, Antonio López de Santa Ana, who looked favorably upon them. Padre Martínez served on various occasions in the Mexican Departmental Assembly for New Mexico and later in the United States Territorial Assembly.

Padre Martínez's interest in politics had, at times, unexpected and tragic consequences for him. In 1837, possibly inspired by his protests against taxation by the Mexican government, the people of Chimayó rose in rebellion, marched on Santa Fe, occupied it, and executed the Governor, Albino Pérez. The rebels were quickly expelled from Santa Fe by troops under the command of Manuel Armijo, and their leaders were executed.

Possibly saddened and chastened by these events, Padre Martínez returned to Taos and vigorously pursued his teaching and ecclesiastical activities. The 1840s in New Mexico witnessed the steadily growing stream of Anglo-Americans coming down the Santa Fe Trail, opened by Mexico in 1821, and the result, almost predictable, was the war against Mexico in 1846.

The coming to power of the United States in what would later be called the American Southwest brought Padre Martínez into contact and confrontation with the new civil and military authorities as well as with the new ecclesiastical authorities of a Catholic Church under American jurisdiction. Fluent in English and fully aware of the needs of his students to be fluent in that language and to understand American written law, Padre Martínez was able to respond positively and constructively to the new presence while still upholding the language, customs, and rights of the Indo-Hispanic people.

When some natives of Taos rose in rebellion and executed Governor Charles Bent, the first American Governor of New Mexico, Padre Martínez was falsely accused of leading the uprising. The accusations came from men like Carlos Beaubien and Ceran St. Vrain who, along with Bent, apparently hated Padre Martínez for opposing their attempts, ultimately successful, to acquire huge land grants in the waning period of Mexican rule in New Mexico. Since there was no evidence to support the accusations, nothing ever came of them. It is interesting to note, however, that Padre Martínez courageously opposed the punitive executions that followed the Taos uprising. In letters written to Manuel Alvarez, a merchant in Santa Fe, and Colonel Sterling Price, in charge of the military, Padre Martínez attacked the injustice of the policy of carrying out the executions. He had great respect for the new American government and he admired the democratic liberal institutions of the United States, but he was not on that account afraid to confront civil and military authorities when he thought it was necessary for the public good.

The American presence was to also bring Padre Martínez into an unexpected confrontation with the new ecclesiastical authority. Jean Baptiste Lamy became, in 1851, the first bishop of the newly created Archdiocese of Santa Fe. Despite his best efforts to remain on good terms with the new bishop, Padre Martínez was not able to support the stands taken by Bishop Lamy on tithing, the rights and the proper role of the native clergy, and matters of canon law. The differences between the two men were complicated by personality clashes and, above all, by the different attitudes the two clergymen had toward the native New Mexicans. Padre Martínez saw himself as the defender of native Indo-Hispanic rights while Bishop Lamy considered the Indo-Hispanics to be inferior in many respects to the Anglo-Americans. An offer of resignation in 1856 by the ailing Padre Martínez that carried with it the condition that the padre be allowed to select his own successor was accepted by Bishop Lamy, although he ignored the attached condition. Misunderstanding of the language and intent may have played a role here. Whether they did or not, the result was that Bishop Lamy excommunicated Padre Martínez between 1858 and 1860. The exact date is unknown because as Fray Angelico Chavez has pointed out in his biography of Padre Martínez, *But Time and Chance,* the bishop left no official record of the excommunication.[1]

Despite the excommunication, Padre Martínez refused to acknowledge its validity and continued to serve as the priest of Taos until the end of his life. He remained a significant figure in the life of the Indo-Hispanic community and continued to meet its religious needs within the institutional church and also by means of his association with the grass-roots lay religious organization known as la Santa Hermandad de Nuestro Padre Jesús, the Holy Brotherhood of Our Lord Jesus Christ the Nazarene, popularly known as the Penitentes because of the acts of self-flagellation and other penitential rites performed by members of the brotherhood during Holy Week. Some observers, like Father Thomas J. Steele and Rowena A. Rivera, point to a possibly very strong organizational role assumed by Padre Martínez with the Penitentes.[2] In any case, the Penitentes gave Padre Martínez the funeral services of a hero.

Several issues concerned me as I set about trying to develop a stage presentation based on Padre Martínez and the critical issues concerning his place in history. I wanted to be as accurate as possible in the portrayal of Padre Martínez on stage. Yet it was obvious from the outset that historical accuracy was not enough. While it was possible to develop a dramatic monologue based on what was known about Padre Martínez—his birth in Abiquiu and childhood in Taos, the tragic death of his wife, his subsequent religious studies in Durango, and so on—a stage model that adhered strictly to historical sources would have virtually to ignore the popular and scholarly impact of Willa Cather's *Death Comes for the Archbishop*.

Beyond a small number of scholars and students of history who take a special interest in all aspects of the Padre Martínez story, few people outside New Mexico would ever have heard of Padre Martínez had it not been for Willa Cather. I did not think that a mere recounting of what was historically known about Padre Martínez, no matter how I chose to dramatize the material, would be sufficient to deal with the larger issues raised by Cather.

Death Comes for the Archbishop is a "narrative," as Cather referred to it,[3] that combines fictional devices and elements with historical references. I refer to it as a hybrid novel precisely because it juxtaposes historical events and personalities in a novelistic contextual form. While this approach to writing a narrative may be an interesting literary experiment, perhaps even a forerunner of the contemporary docudrama, it does leave Willa Cather open to both literary and historical criticism.

Hybrid novel or narrative, it remains to this day immensely popular, no small tribute to Cather's literary skills; it is still one of the first introductions of literate Americans to New Mexico and the Southwest. Willa Cather's Padre Martínez is (1) a dark priest, (2) a dictator in his priestly realm, (3) an instigator of rebellion against the United States, (4) a betrayer of the Taos Indians, (5) a thief who enriches himself by stealing Indian lands, (6) a relic from the past, (7) a brutal, insensitive man, (8) a filthy, slovenly man, (9) an animal-like man with yellow eyes and long, yellow teeth, and (10) a priest lost in lust and sensuality. The Indians and Mexicans who form the basis of Padre Martínez's society are viewed as (1) childlike in their need for theatricality in their religion, (2) gluttonous, (3) animal-like in their sensuality, (4) barbaric, and (5) savage.

So powerful and compelling is Cather's indictment of Padre Martínez, so brilliantly developed is her theme of a Catholic Church fallen upon evil days under Spanish and Mexican jurisdiction, and so widely read is *Death Comes for the Archbishop,* that I thought it necessary to grant Padre Martínez an opportunity to have his day in court; to be able to reply to his two principal detractors, Archbishop Jean Baptiste Lamy and Willa Cather.

As a historian, my presentation on stage, *Padre Antonio José Martíne*z *of Taos,* forced me to examine my basic approaches to history. Over a period of five years, I groped, intuited, and thought my way to an understanding of what I was doing on stage. I felt uncomfortable, as a historian, to have to deviate even slightly from conclusions that could be derived from historical evidence. Nevertheless, in the case of Padre Martínez and probably in all historical cases, any stage presentation would have to take serious liberties with the evidence of the primary source materials. Try as I might, I could not enter into the bygone reality of Padre Martínez. I rejected out of hand any possibility of historical empathy as an occupational delusion of historians. I could harvest the bare-bone facts of Padre Martínez's past experience, but I would still be processing that information through my own mind. And my mind, in addition to whatever genetic codes might be imprinted on it, had been formed in a twentieth-century urban environment totally unknown to Padre Martínez.

Haltingly, then, I worked toward a presentation that would balance four critical factors in having Padre Martínez confront Willa Cather and, to a lesser extent, Archbishop Jean Baptiste Lamy, on stage. (1) I wanted to be as accurate as possible in reference to historical data about Padre Martínez. (2) I wanted to be as accurate as possible in the use of historical data related to Archbishop Jean Baptiste Lamy. (3) I wanted to be as historically accurate as possible in all references to Willa Cather. (4) I wanted to use the elements of drama to provide an entertaining as well as informative presentation on stage. My task, as I saw it, was to create a fantasy on stage, taking the necessary fictional liberties, that would provide a milieu within which an alternative view of the historical significance of Padre Martínez could be presented. Since I knew from experience that history is an attempted reconstruction of the past beset by pitfalls everywhere, I had to ask myself hard questions about my basic views of history and historiography and about my own philosophy of history.

What I developed, then, over the course of five years, from 1982 to 1987, was an approach to history that respected "everyday experience," i.e., the life blood of history, but amplified that historical reality through the use of imaginative processes, which themselves are part of human psychological experience—without which there can be no understanding of history. Robbed of the imaginative links that make it a comprehensible reconstruction of the past, history is reduced to a tiresome and meaningless chronology. I took this process of imaginative linkage one step further to bring Padre Antonio José Martínez, Archbishop Jean Baptiste Lamy, and Willa Cather together on the stage; this made it possible for Padre Martínez to "reply" to Archbishop Lamy, who was at least a contemporary, and also "reply" to Willa Cather, whose lifespan (1873–1947) did not coincide with that of the padre (1793–1867).

As I constructed my one-man one-act play about Padre Martínez, I had more to be concerned about than the juxtaposition of historically asynchronous personalities. However faithful I might try to be to the historical evidence concerning my three principal characters, I also deemed it necessary to construct a stage piece that would have merit on its own terms as a work of theater.

The stage, in effect, has its own concerns. Any empty space will do as a theater, but in that "empty space" (a term coined, I believe, by Peter Brook),[4] action, movement, tension, and a resolution to that tension must occur if there is to be any theater at all. While lighting, costuming, and set design are important to good theater, these were not my major concerns. With one character on stage (Padre Martínez), and minimal staging effects achieved with one chair (if one was available), and learning to make do with whatever lighting effects, if any, might be available on the road, I designed my performance to be highly flexible in terms of being able to adapt immediately to whatever conditions I might encounter in the small towns and villages of New Mexico.

I have always believed in the power of the stage to unleash the creative imaginative forces of both audience and playwright. A simple priest's cassock was sufficient for a "costume," and a single chair on stage would do for a stage setting. I liked the chair on stage as a device for focusing audience attention. Who was going to sit in that chair? Who was going to be on the "hot spot" where he could be subjected to the close scrutiny of the audience? The chair, in short, enhanced my primary goal of focusing audience attention for a reconsideration of Padre Martínez.

Simplicity of staging and presentation was the key to my approach to dealing with the problems of having a priest, long dead, address a contemporary of his, the archbishop, and a noncontemporary author, both long dead. Simplicity made it possible for me to remain conscious, as a historian, of what was history in my presentation and what was theater, with its needs for action, transitions, and dramatic tension and resolution.

Whatever the dramatic needs of my one-act play, the entire enterprise would have struck me as futile if history were not the key factor in the presentation. If drama were the technique and the form, history had to be the motive force, the machine that drove the drama. As mentioned above, however, theater has its own concerns, and they must be respected.

Would Padre Martínez have reacted the way I depict him on stage if he had had the opportunity to reply to Willa Cather? No one, of course, can answer that question. It strikes me, however, that a model based on projections greatly at variance with what we know about Padre Martínez would certainly elicit a negative response. Indeed, this is precisely the response Willa Cather's character has elicited from many people who are familiar with Southwest history and particularly the historic circumstances related to Padre Martínez. More important, however, my approach, while historiographically sound, allows for a flexible examination of a multiplicity of informed views. Such an examination may help clarify and inform our view of the time/space-bound sequential past that shapes the fleeting moment of life that is forever moving into the future.

There are seventeen scenes in this play. A good director should be able to shorten or entirely omit some of the scenes depending on conditions or time constraints. Between the historical sequences, I insert fictional interludes that allow Padre Martínez to address the audience about his reactions to Willa Cather and Archbishop Lamy. Scene 17 allows me to give Padre Martínez a holistic world view that

I think is in keeping with what we know historically about the man.

The play opens with the obviously fictional device of Padre Martínez reflecting on his surroundings (a not unreasonable thing to do for someone who has just awakened from the dead) and then moving on to a consideration of his early life circumstances. Here I review his birth into the large Martínez family at Abiquiu in 1793 and the subsequent family move to Taos in 1804. I then pass on to the first fictional sequence, which allows Padre Martínez to address directly the charges of lust and fathering of illegitimate children that Willa Cather levels at him in *Death Comes for the Archbishop*. Given that there are probably unanswerable historical questions about Padre Martínez in this context, I have my fictional padre take the edge off Cather's charges, although not necessarily negate them entirely.

From the third through the sixth scenes, I have Padre Martínez review some of the major events in his life as we know them from primary sources. I have Padre Martínez talk about his adolescence, his youthful arranged marriage to María de la Luz and her untimely death. I take the minimum necessary fictional liberties in these scenes to portray a multidimensional human being. Thus, for example, while nothing has been discovered in the historic records so far to indicate that Padre Martínez reacted to his wife's death with great sorrow, it is not an unreasonable assumption that he expressed sorrow. There is certainly nothing in the historical sources to indicate that he was a man of no affect.

Padre Martínez on stage then reviews his years in the Tridentine Seminary in Durango, Mexico, the political turmoil of Mexico, and the example of enlightened nineteenth-century liberalism and concern for social justice set by Padre Miguel Hidalgo, the leader of Mexican independence from Spain. I concentrate on Padre Martínez's political liberalism because I think it was one of the key factors that alienated him from the politically conservative Archbishop Lamy.

Subsequent scenes show Padre Martínez returning to New Mexico in 1823 to practice his vocation, to deal with his personal loss at the death of his daughter in 1824, and to become the Curate of Taos in 1826. I try to show a vigorous Padre Martínez who, having been deprived of both wife and child, plunges into a swirl of ecclesiastical, educational, and political activity. The context is the 1830s and the 1840s, the years that saw the opening of his school, the seminary in Taos, the use of his printing press to publish educational and religious materials, and his involvement as a champion of liberal causes in New Mexico politics, which first the War of the Chimayosos and later the Yankee invasion of Mexico complicated unduly. It is also within this context that I insert a heavily fictionalized scene in which I hint that there may have been a serious gap in Padre Martínez's personal life, a gap that may or may not have been filled by doña Teodora Romero (the historical record is not entirely clear on this matter and is subject to various interpretations).

From the tenth scene to the fourteenth, I review in Padre Martínez's monologue the 1837 uprising in northern New Mexico against the Mexican government (*la guerra de los chimayosos*), the American invasion in 1846 of what had been Mexican territory, and last but not least, the historical confrontation with Archbishop Lamy.

Contrary to the view advanced by Willa Cather, historical records indicate that there were complex cultural and political differences underlying the dispute between the two priests. Archbishop Lamy stood for the major tradition within the Church, the tradition of Rome and the splendid edifice of medieval philosophy that was at one time the very core of European civilization and culture. Padre Martínez, on the other hand, while he was a part of that major tradition, more accurately reflected the minor tradition of local Mexican and Indo-Hispanic influence at the fringe of the European world view. For Archbishop Lamy, the French Revolution was a negative force in human history, while for Padre Martínez the era of liberalism partially heralded by the French Revolution was the dawn of a new day of liberty. Archbishop Lamy had neither the cultural sensitivity to his Spanish speaking flock nor the humility to recognize that a unique interplay of Spanish, Mexican, and Indian cultures had evolved over time in New Mexico and that these cultures were valuable in and of themselves. I do not think it is being too harsh on the Archbishop to point out his own French and European ethnocentricity in his approach to his new archdiocese.

One dispute followed another, as I point out in the monologue on stage, disputes over tithing, over the construction of a new cathedral, and over the role of la Santa Hermandad de Nuestro Padre Jesús, better known as the Penitentes. The archbishop needed revenues for a new stone cathedral, while Padre Martínez was very much aware of the barter nature of the New Mexican economy. The archbishop was fearful of the Santa Hermandad, while Padre Martínez was deeply involved in its structure and ceremonies. When Padre Martínez offered to resign as Curate of Taos on the condition that he be allowed to prepare his successor for carrying out the parish tasks, Archbishop Lamy, deliberately or otherwise, accepted the resignation and ignored the condition. The culmination of these events occurred between 1858 and 1860, as indicated earlier, when Archbishop Lamy excommunicated Padre Martínez from the Church.

As I point out on stage, Padre Martínez ignored the excommunication, quite probably with good cause, and continued to be the parish priest of Taos until his death in 1867. In my final scene on stage, one almost entirely fictional, I have Padre Martínez revealing his stoical Christian philosophy as expressed in his Relación De Méritos Del Presbitero Antonio José Martínez, taken from Ecclesiastes 9:11: "I returned, and saw under the sun, that the race is not to the swift, nor the battle to the strong . . . but time and chance happeneth to them all."[5] Then I have Padre Martínez go off somewhere in the mists of metaphysical speculation searching for Willa Cather, with whom he would "like to discuss theory of fiction as compared to theory of history." (I could not resist having Padre Martínez make a historiographic commentary by this time.) He is also off in search of Archbishop Lamy, with whom he "would like to discuss certain matters of Canon Law." In his parting vision on stage, I have Padre Martínez make comments to the effect that it is through "time and chance" that we learn to heal the wounds we inflict on one another in our earthly sojourn. My readings in primary and secondary sources on Padre Martínez impressed me with the idea that here was basically a kindly and loving man who was also highly intelligent, independent in thought, and very vigorous. This parting gesture, then, appears to me to be in keeping with Padre Martínez's historic character as a priest and as a man.

Over the course of more than four years, I presented my dramatization of Padre Martínez to audiences in New Mexico, Arizona, Texas, Colorado, and Nebraska. One of the high points of this period occurred when *The New York Times* of June 29, 1985, published an article on my performance written by Iver Peterson, at that time Denver bureau chief for the *Times*. I have never considered this kind of dramatization as any kind of substitute for solid archival research. This experience has, however, led me to probe more deeply than ever before into the enigmas and limitations of time, space, and the historical evidence of bygone human existence. It has also encouraged me to try to develop models of history that may enable future historians to probe more deeply the multiple dimensions of the human condition as revealed in history.

Throughout the years of my research and writing efforts, I have been very much aware of the work of others who have labored with great love and care to provide us with an accurate historic portrait of Padre Antonio José Martínez of Taos. There are several writers, in particular, who deserve special mention. Fray Angelico Chavez with his biography of Padre Martínez, *But Time And Chance,* and Paul Horgan with his biography of Archbishop Jean Baptiste Lamy, *Lamy of Santa Fe,* have enriched my experience of the reading of history as they have for many. Also the numerous works of Father Thomas Steele, S.J., most notably *Penitente Self-Government,* written with Rowena A. Rivera, and his other books related to New Mexico Catholicism, have been most beneficial to me in my own reading and research. I would also like to mention Ray John de Aragón whose book, *Padré Martínez and Bishop Lamy,* is a pioneer work that closely compares these two historical figures. While I conceived independently the idea of using Willa Cather's reference to the "children" of Padre Martínez as a means of bringing into my play the Spanish *"hijos"* which, like its English counterpart, can have the double meaning of *children* in the pastoral as well as the biological sense, Ray John de Aragón was the first writer to publish the expression by Padre Martínez, *"estos son mis hijos,"* in a somewhat different context, in his book mentioned above. I am indebted to these and to many other persons who have enlightened me with their insights, suggestions, conversations, goodwill, and support of all kind.

Notes

1. Fray Angelico Chavez, *But Time And Chance* (Santa Fe: Sunstone Press, 1981), p. 150.

2. Thomas J. Steele, S.J., and Rowena A. Rivera, *Penitente Self-Government* (Santa Fe: Ancient City Press, 1985), pp. 19–23.

3. James Woodress, *Willa Cather Her Life And Art* (Lincoln: University of Nebraska Press, 1970), p. 220.

4. Peter Brook, *The Empty Space* (New York: Avon Books, 1968).

5. Read Collection. Antonio José Martínez. *Relación De Meritos Del Presbitero Antonio José Martínez, Domiciliario Del Obispado De Durango, Cura Encargado De Taos En El Departamento De Nuevo México* (Taos: Impresa en su oficina a cargo de Jesús María Baca, 1838), p. 1.

I

RETURNED
AND SAW
UNDER THE SUN

PADRE MARTÍNEZ OF TAOS

The Character:
Padre Antonio José Martínez, the priest of Taos

The Setting:
Padre Martínez, in this play, is given the opportunity to return from the dead and answer the "charges" that have been addressed to him by history and by circumstance. Specifically, Padre Martínez wants to answer the historical ghosts of Archbishop Jean Baptiste Lamy, first bishop and later archbishop of Santa Fe, and Willa Cather, who took Padre Martínez so cruelly to task in her celebrated novel, Death Comes For The Archbishop.

Staging is minimal in order to allow for maximum flexibility and minimum cost in performing as a travelling play. The number of scenes is also flexible to allow for shorter performances with proper editing (see introduction) or for a full performance. Dressed in a priest's cassock, or suitable facsimile of a priest's garment, the character enters a pool of light near stage center. The character may enter from either stage left or stage right. Slightly off center stage toward stage right is a chair, the only prop on stage. If lighting is available, a red backdrop with sub-

dued red footlights provides a good ambience for the play. Padre Martínez will play slightly downstage of the prop and will use it as indicated by the stage directions given or as modified by the director.

I

Enter PADRE MARTÍNEZ. *He is aged and bent, lost in deep thought. He walks slowly toward stage center, walks past the chair, then slowly returns to it and sits down, facing the audience.*

PADRE MARTÍNEZ (*makes the sign of the cross or clasps his hands as if in prayer; rouses himself as if from deep meditation*):

> *¿Qué es la vida?, un frenesí;*
> *¿Qué es la vida?, una ilusión,*
> *una sombra, una ficción,*
> *y el mayor bien es pequeño;*
> *que toda la vida es sueño*
> *y los sueños, sueños son.*

Palabras del gran poeta y dramaturgo, Calderón de la Barca. Oh, yes, I understand that I should use the language of the new dispensation, *el inglés.* I was saying that these words I muttered are the words of a great poet and playwright, Calderón de la Barca. What is life?, he asks. A frenzy. An illusion. A shadow, a fiction. And the greatest good, all that we accomplish, is small because life is a dream. And dreams are only dreams.

Now I return from the dream time to share my ambitions, my victories, my defeats, my dreams with you. We move from dream to dream in our celestial voyage. We are ambitious. Our ambitions prosper or they turn to ashes. We have our victories. We see them turn to defeats and in the midst of defeat we snatch an unexpected victory. One dream ends and another one begins. We move from dream to dream seeking the light that will light our way to another dream. And time and chance are the gamblers who play with our fate from dream to dream. They always deal from the bottom of the deck, or so it seems to us who are not given the gift of knowing the forces of light and darkness that guide these celestial gamblers. Yet we have our faith to keep us strong through the darkest times.

2

(He rouses himself from the chair, looks over his shoulder upstage and stage right. He looks in this direction when he addresses the invisible ghosts of Archbishop Lamy and Willa Cather.) I know they're listening out there in the mists somewhere. Those two. *Esa mujer.* That woman. What was her name? Willa. Yes, Willa. Willa Cather. And the good bishop! I hope I shall find them soon. There are a good many things I would like to discuss with them. *¡Ay, qué mujer!* What a woman!

The terrible things she said about me in that novel of hers, *Death Comes for the Archbishop.*

(He paces back and forth, occasionally muttering to himself in between his direct addresses to the audience.)

She said that I had long, yellow teeth. She said that I lusted after women. Well, have you ever known a man who didn't lust after women? And, oh yes, she said that I had all those children. It's too bad Willa didn't know me *como un hombre de carne y hueso,* as a man of flesh and bone, as we say in Spanish. She might have found me less colorful, less picaresque.

It's too bad Willa didn't know the good bishop. She might have found him not quite the plaster saint she portrayed him to be in that novel of hers. He was, rather, a staunch defender of the Church in his own right but so stubborn and so lacking in understanding of *los nuevomexicanos.*

Do you hear that, Bishop Lamy? I said *lacking in understanding.* You can't get out of that one. And you, Willa, what did you really know about my children?

3

(He turns toward the audience.) Oh, I haven't forgotten about my children. I know you've been wondering about that. *(He sits at the chair.)* Well, let me tell you about my children. There were many of them.

When I think of my children, I can still see them seated at their rude log benches in the one room school I had for them in Taos—my very own living room.

(He rises and moves a few paces stage right and occasionally gestures toward a space on stage right that is his "school." The director has great freedom in staging this kind of scene.)

I would watch over my children as they studied. I taught them in their native language, of course, *el español,* and I taught them the catechism, spelling, mathematics, all that I thought would be useful for them in a rapidly changing world. I also taught my children *en el inglés,* in English, *por si acaso,* just in case that friendly giant to the north, *los Estados Unidos,* should decide to become less friendly.

I also taught my children something of the law. You know, we Spanish-speaking *nuevomexicanos,* we Mexicans and Spaniards and half-breeds, for most of us were part Indian, we had a saying in Spanish: *es hombre de su palabra.* He is a man of his word. I knew, however, that under the Anglo-American law the written word was of supreme importance. So I taught my children about the American law. I used to say to them: *La nación americana es un burro en que van montados los abogados.* The American nation is a donkey ridden by lawyers. Do you know what it is to have to deal with lawyers? Well, I didn't like dealing with them and so I became one, an ecclesiastical attorney. *(Turning over his shoulder)* Isn't that right, Bishop Lamy? Is that why you were so fearful of a direct confrontation with me? Did you suspect the weakness of your case against me? How advantageous for you that I was aged and infirm in my time of troubles with you. Otherwise, with my knowledge of ecclesiastical law ... well, who knows how things might have gone? *(Turning back toward the audience)* I did everything I could, in short, to try to prepare my children for the certainty of change. Oh, I took great pride in my children. I worked as hard at trying to educate them as I am tonight trying to educate you! *(Said to the audience) Uds. son mis hijos.* Your are my children! Just as much as my students were in that long-ago Taos of the last century. How could Willa Cather have accused me of being the physical father of my own students? And so many of them. *Ay qué mujer. (Turning over his right shoulder to address Willa)* You have some views to answer for, Willa. Was it really so important to your novel that you had to give credence to one of the most shopworn charges that can be leveled against a priest, almost any priest? *¡Qué mujer!* Someday, Willa, we must meet and discuss these matters.

4

(Turning back toward the audience) Oh, I don't want you to misunderstand me. I'm not going to stand here before you, in this moment of trial, pretending to some imagined virtue. I wasn't born to be a priest, you know. When I was born in Abiquiu in 1793 and then moved to Taos in 1804 with my father, don Antonio Severino, and my mother, doña María

del Carmen Santistéban, I wasn't raised a priest. I was born to be a *vaquero*. What you would call a cowboy, a *ranchero al estilo norteño,* a rancher in the style of northern New Mexico.

Why, when I was only this high, I could ride a fast horse as well as any young *vaquero* in the north. We had this game we used to play. A game we had taught the Indians. It was called *el gallo,* the rooster. We would take a rooster and bury it up to its neck in sand. Then we would form a semi-circle with our horses around the rooster, ride in as fast as we could, swoop down over the saddle horn and grab the rooster by the neck, jerking it up out of the sand. *Al gallo no le gustaba.* The rooster didn't like it. A rough and a cruel game you say. Yes, but those were rough and occasionally cruel times on the Taos frontier in the early 1800s.

And so I passed my youth, learning all the trades of a *vaquero,* of a *ranchero,* for as the first-born son I knew that some day I would inherit my father's ranch and his possessions and I would have to become a good steward of what would be entrusted to me. I enjoyed the roping and the riding, the branding of cattle. How could I ever forget the sight of the arrival of one of my father's caravans after completing the arduous journey from Mexico City and Chihuahua. The carts, *las carretas,* were stuffed with the staples we so desperately needed on the frontier—iron nails, so rare and such a luxury, hand tools, dishes, rare spices, silverware, fine leather goods, so many things we so often had to do without, and the few luxuries that we could afford in this land where there was practically no money to speak of!

5

So I passed my time of youth. One day, my father, don Antonio Severino, came to me and he brought with him a young lass. When I saw the way her dark tresses cascaded down over her shoulder and breast, I was drawn to her. We became fast friends. In the evenings we would take long walks beneath the brilliant Taos sky. We thought that sky was only ours, as so many lovers have thought, long before our time, and long before the time of those artists who, at a later date, were to make Taos so well known for its sky and mountains. It was as if a new light had come into my life. Indeed, that was her name. María de la Luz, or Mary of the Light. We were soon married. It was an arranged marriage, yes, for such was our custom. But it seemed to work as well as your non-arranged marriages of a late time.

For one brief year, I enjoyed all the bliss associated with the marital state. At the end of that year it came time for María de la Luz to give birth. We didn't have the kind of medicine you have today, you know, and in the moment of childbirth we lost my wife. We did what we could to save the life of our infant daughter and we did save her life. We named her María de la Luz in honor of her mother.

In my sorrow at such a great loss, I turned to the Holy Bible, *la santa biblia,* seeking consolation. The more I read in these sacred texts, the more I began to wonder whether or not I had a vocation for the priesthood. I wrote to the bishop in Durango. He wrote back. The correspondence went on for four years and the bishop urged me to ride south, to leave my family and enter the seminary to see whether or not I had a vocation for the priesthood.

6

(He walks to extreme stage right and slowly works his way back toward stage center during the following monologue.)

You know, it is still winter in the months of February and March in Taos. And it was on such a cold day at that time of year in 1817 that I bade a fond farewell to don Antonio Severino and doña María del Carmen Santistéban and also to little María de la Luz, who was beginning to blossom into young girlhood. It was a sad and tender moment as I embraced them, my father and my mother, my daughter, and I knew I would not see them for many long years. But there was a crispness in the air that morning and I knew that the years ahead would be years of excitement as well as education. Years of adventure for this young *nuevomexicano* who had heard so many tales of Mexico from the caravan fleet drivers who were employed in my father's trade business along the Chihuahua trail.

And so I left Taos. I followed the sacred river, what we called el Río Bravo, or el Río del Norte, or el Río Grande, as it is known today, south, south to Santa Fe, the city of holy faith, and then on down through Alburquerque. I understand that Alburquerque has lost one of those "r's" over the years. I continued on south through Belen, the village of Bethlehem, and then on to Socorro. Don't we often need succor in our lives? Then I rode further south through San Antonio and then through the town we used to call Las Palomas, or "the doves." An attractive name, right? Later, I understand, the *americanos* changed that to Hot Springs. That's also a nice name. Then I understand that many years after my death there was this new invention, this electric thing, the radio, and then there was some kind of program, *no sé qué,* a radio program, and the people of the village changed the name of Hot Springs to Truth or Consequences. *(He shakes his head in great disbelief.)* I always was a liberal in the classic, nineteenth-century tradition. I always believed in change and progress. But sometimes, one does wonder. I continued my journey south. I rode through El Paso del Norte. There was no Ciudad Juárez at that time. Then I rode on to Chihuahua and Durango.

7

You should have seen Mexico in those days. For Mexico was aflame with revolution. Mexico was in the full throes of rebellion against the *gachupín,* the occupying Spaniard. Well, I entered the seminary and began my studies in theology and metaphysics. I admit it was difficult at times for me to pay attention to my studies for there was much happening in politics all around me.

Throughout Mexico, in the great cities, you could hear

the slogans of the French Revolution: *¡Libertad, Justicia, Igualdad!* Liberty, Justice, and Equality. It was all so stirring. I was still a young man in those days and I thought a new day of liberty was at hand. The United States to the north had already established a liberal democracy and now Mexico seemed ready to embark on a similar course. Alas, I was to learn all too soon that when those grand slogans of revolution are shouted through the streets, bloodshed is certain to follow.

What I want you to remember, though, is that I learned my politics not from the words of politicians but rather from the remembered words of the great leader of Mexican independence, Padre Miguel Hidalgo. Yes it was from the remembered words of a great priest, Padre Miguel Hidalgo, that I learned that a priest can care for the well being of his flock, his parishioners, his *children,* here and now as well as in the great realm to come after death.

So, it was with some difficulty that I paid attention to my studies under these most stimulating circumstances. I did well enough in my studies, however, to take highest honors and even though this cough that seems to have pursued me beyond the grave bothered me continually, I still enjoyed the celebrations when Mexico achieved its independence from Spain in 1821. The cough grew worse, however, and my superiors feared I had not long to live. As I said earlier, we didn't have the kind of medicine you have today. It was decided by my superiors, then, to ordain me a priest in 1822, just shortly before my thirtieth birthday. Since my grades had been so high and my health was not very promising, I was granted a dispensation from my last year of studies and ordained a priest about one year short of completing my formal studies.

8

When I rode back north, I observed the dry, dusty villages that dotted the northern provinces of Mexico. Everywhere there was poverty. Everywhere there was a strong faith and a fierce and joyful love of life. Everywhere time and chance, those great gamblers and arbiters of our fate, had dealt to the people from the bottom of the deck and yet they held fast to their way of living, to their land, and to their hopes for a better life in this harsh and beautiful land. They held fast to their dreams in this desert country where dreams are part of the very landscape.

There to greet me as I rode into Taos were my father and mother, and María de la Luz, now a delightful eleven year old. Well, as you can imagine, it was a wonderful moment for me. I began practicing my vocation as a priest. I baptized our infants shortly after they were born. I married our youngsters when that time came. And I buried our dead in the *camposanto,* the holy ground, when that time came as it must come to all of us.

This was a joyful time for me. My church duties kept me very busy but I still had time to spend with my lovely young daughter. I enjoyed every spare moment that allowed me to take my fast horse and ride across the Taos plains to Ranchitos, where María de la Luz was being raised by her grandparents in my father's great *rancho*. So time passed in that one joyful year.

Too soon, all too soon, this good time moved on to the realm of dreams. The year was 1824 and one of those terrible fevers swept through the land. As I've told you, we didn't have the kind of medicine you of a later time have come to take for granted. One evening, a dark rider came from my father's rancho.

"Come quickly, padre," he said to me. "It's your daughter. She's very sick."

I took my fastest horse and galloped across the plain only to arrive too late. She was twelve years old when she died.

9

Well what's a man to do? *(He strides back and forth somewhat nervously during this scene. The pacing of his delivery here is much faster than is usually the case.)* I continued to be the good priest of Taos. I baptized our infants, married our youngsters, and buried our dead in the *camposanto*. I bought a printing press from that fellow, Ramón Abreu, down in Santa Fe, and I began to publish religious tracts as well as a newspaper, *The Dawn of Liberty* I called it, where I was able to address my political concerns for the poor and the oppressed. I opened my school in my own home and began to educate our youngsters. I became involved in politics. Three times I ran for the Mexican Departmental Assembly. Three time I was elected. With the approval of Bishop

Zubiría of Durango, I opened a seminary and began to prepare young men for the priesthood. I personally paid for the educational expenses of those students who otherwise would not have been able to attend my school. I did everything I could, in short, to try to fill the long, empty hours left to me after losing both wife and daughter. And still the days and nights were long and empty and the winters cold and miserable.

This would have been a far more terrible time had it not been for doña Teodora Romero, my housekeeper. She swept and mopped the church, prepared my meals, ironed my cassocks, and her good humor was a constant encouragement to me. But ah!, I don't want to give rise to scandal. *(Turning over his shoulder to address Willa off in the mists at stage right)* You would see doña Teodora in the most evil light, wouldn't you Willa? *¡Qué lástima!* What a shame that you had such an eye for scandal in that novel of yours. We must surely discuss this issue. *(Turning back toward the audience)* *¡Qué mujer!* In any case, doña Teodora was a good woman and—but I don't want to give rise to scandal. Merely let me say that she served the Church well and assisted this humble priest in going about his duties.

Time and chance continued to bring new dangers, new opportunities into my life. The Mexican government named me consul at Taos because of my command of English. I kept a cold eye on the constant arrival of so many *americanos*. I knew it had been a mistake for the Mexican government to open the Santa Fe Trail in 1821. I tried to warn my government, as so many did, that our frontiers were over-extended and the *americanos* were penetrating our beloved Mexico all along the northern tier of our territories. Naturally I opposed the efforts of wealthy *americanos* to acquire land grants by forming blind partnerships with unsuspecting, or greedy, *mexicanos*. Mexico in its desperate need to gain revenues consented to these tragic land grants that helped prepare the way for the invasion of the *americanos*.

IO

The years quickly passed. It was 1837 and the Mexican government, always trying to raise revenues, imposed a new tax on the northern territories. I opposed such a move because I knew how poor our people were. Of course, I understood and sympathized with the plight of Mexico. Torn apart by civil wars in the Yucatán and in Texas (although why anyone would want Texas I don't know), the infant Republic of Mexico needed money in order to raise the troops who would supposedly suppress these various separatist tendencies. I sympathized with Mexico, yes, but I knew there was no spare money to be raised in New Mexico. Do you know how hard it is to make money or raise money in New Mexico? As I said, I opposed the new tax and I sent a letter protesting this unwarranted tax to that newspaper *La Gaceta* in Santa Fe.

My words struck a spark I had not intended. Soon the farmers and ranchers of the valley of Santa Cruz, the people of Chimayó, refused to pay the tax and rose in rebellion against the Mexican government. And although it was weak, the Mexican government still had sufficient strength to send its dragoons to the northern frontier. It was a brief, farcical, and tragic war, as all wars are tragic. The rebels marched on Santa Fe, took the city and executed the governor, Albino Pérez. By early 1838, the Mexican troops under the command of that young upstart from Alburquerque, Manuel Armijo, had driven the rebels out of Santa Fe. Some were executed. Some fled back to their native villages and pueblos.

Sickened and saddened by such bloodshed, I returned to my parish in Taos wanting to have nothing to do with politics again. For a man of my temperament, though, it was difficult to stay out of politics. Well, for one thing, there was that problem with the *tejanos,* those Texans. Under the guise of wanting to trade with us, they actually invaded New Mexico in 1841 and 1843. We trounced them and sent them reeling back to Texas. Those Texans never fooled me. I saw their "Republic of Texas" as a mere pretext for the United States to invade and take over our lands. I did what I could to stir the people to action, to repel the invaders and protect themselves.

Actually, it wasn't so much the Texans I feared, although they were a crude lot and most unfriendly to our native *nuevomexicanos.* No it wasn't so much the Texans as that lurking giant to the north that had spawned Texas and would later reabsorb it. *Los Estados Unidos.*

II

(He turns over his shoulder, upstage and stage right, to address Bishop Lamy) And you, Bishop Lamy, how did you see *Los Estados Unidos?* Now here you had come all the way from France to find yourself far away from those liberal democratic movements of Europe you so intensely disliked. You had no use for the French Revolution. You had seen much of the social status and political power of the Church destroyed by that revolution. Farmer boy that you were, raised in rural southern France, you grew up as a political conservative. Just like the vast majority of priests at that time. Then you came to New Mexico carrying the full weight of your conservatism on your back. I wonder what you really thought of that liberal democracy to the north, *Los Estados Unidos?* Did you really admire the United States that much or did you merely contrast its obvious political and military strength with that of Mexico? *(sadly)* I know what a low opinion you had of our *nuevomexicanos.*

(He turns back toward the audience) My own feelings toward the United States were quite mixed. I admired their Constitution, their separation of church and state, their democratic elections and, in general, the great well of liberal philosophy from which the United States had sprung. Indeed, I was so pleased to see my beloved Mexico model its institutions after those of the United States.

(He paces nervously back and forth, occasionally sitting down for a few moments in the chair.)

There were also many things I didn't like about the United States. I couldn't stand their land-grabbing greed. That is why I opposed all their attempts to seize control of our land base. No wonder Carlos Bent didn't like me. Or Carlos Beaubien and his son Narciso for that matter. Or Kit Carson. They all saw me as an impediment to their business interests—which was easy enough for them to do since I did not hide my opposition to their interests as they ran counter, in my opinion, to the interests of the Indians and the Mexican population. I didn't like the racial attitudes of many of the *americanos*. I didn't like the arrogance of many of the *americanos* who assumed it was their *manifest destiny* to rule North America from the Atlantic to the Pacific, from the North Pole to the isthmus of Panama, to round out their "natural boundaries," as they called it, on the planet. Now you tell me, what is a "natural boundary" on a globe?

(He sits in the chair.) By the year 1846, I knew that Mexico would not be able to maintain control of its northern provinces. What can I say? I loved Mexico. I also knew its political, military, and economic weaknesses. I knew it had been a terrible mistake for Mexico to open its frontier to free trade with the United States. By opening the Santa Fe Trail I knew my country had invited the rapacious eagle of the north to come dine with the new-born lamb of liberty south of the Arkansas River. The Yankees came by the hundreds and then by the thousands down that trail. And yes, they brought their enticing goods with them, the manufactured goods so superior to those we could obtain from Mexico, and available in such abundance! And Mexico? Well,

long after my time a Mexican general, Porfirio Díaz, that betrayer of Mexican liberalism, I might add, used an expression that could as well have applied to Mexico from the moment of its birth: *"pobre México, tan lejos de Dios y tan cerca de Estados Unidos."* "Poor Mexico, so far from God and so close to the United States." The wealth of the United States was too much of a temptation for many of our *mexicanos* to resist. Members of my own family became fleet drivers along the Santa Fe Trail. Increasingly, members of my own family looked toward St. Louis and other points east rather than south toward Mexico City. Even Governor Manuel Armijo became so involved with business on the Santa Fe Trail that, although his heart remained Mexican, his bank account became American.

I knew that change was coming, that change was inevitable. I was fifty-three years old in 1846. I had lived far longer than anyone had ever thought I would. I had lived long enough to see those two gamblers who are always riding through the dark and obscure roads of destiny, those two gamblers, time and chance, destroy the remnants of the Spanish Empire in the New World. I had lived long enough to see time and chance take both my wife and child from me. And now in my old age, I was seeing time and chance bring these *americanos* in ever larger numbers into *Nuevo México*. Surely, I thought, time and chance have done with me, for I am growing old and my powers are failing me. There is a whirlwind gathering in the north and it is about to descend on us, and I can do nothing except care for my flock with what little strength I have left. Every moment of my life has moved off to the realm of dreams and yet new dreams flow in from the realm of the future. When all is said and done, these dreams are all dreams and they are only dreams. Why do we become so agitated over them? I grew so weary with life.

12

(Suddenly, there is a shift in mood. From somewhere within himself, Padre Martínez finds the strength for a new burst of energy. He rises from the chair and becomes very animated.)

But you know, there's nothing like a stirring speech to get the old juices flowing again. Why, the moment I received a report about the movement of American troops and that speech by their commander, I roused myself. Oh yes, I wasn't caught unawares by the *americanos.* Word came to me that boys dressed in blue had left Bent's Fort on the Arkansas River and were seen coming down through Raton Pass. They were on their way to Santa Fe, of course, and eventually they went all the way to the Pacific. And word came to me what their commander, Colonel Stephen Watts Kearny, said when he entered Las Vegas, the city on the meadows, dividing the plains from the Sangre de Cristo Mountains. Colonel Kearny stood atop the roof of a building near the plaza (and you can still see that building today in Las Vegas), and he addressed the newly created *ciudadanos norteamericanos,* most of whom spoke only a few words

of English, and he said to them: "Not a pepper, not an on-
ion of yours shall I take without your permission." Then
the good colonel promptly added, however, "he who rises
in rebellion against me, him I shall promptly hang." So
much for the tender mercies of our conquerors.

*(He alternates addressing the audience, circling around the chair
as if it were the focal point of his trial, and addressing the ghosts
of Willa Cather and Bishop Lamy.)*

¿Pues qué se podía hacer? What could I do? Of course there
were those among us who counseled military resistance.
(Turning over his shoulder upstage and stage right) What would
you have done, Willa? You with your concern for honor
and the finer things of life? What was I supposed to do as a
loyal citizen of Mexico? Ah yes, and you, Bishop? The great
North American Protestant liberal nation was at hand. How
would you have dealt with this? Given your low opinion of
our people, do you think the coming of the United States
was preferable to Mexican sovereignty, despite the fact that
the Protestant churches were strong in their ranks?

(Turning to the audience) Yes, there were those who counseled military resistance. And let me tell you, if I had
thought for one moment that military resistance could have
saved Mexico's northern provinces from this unwarranted
intrusion, I personally would have led our troops into com-
bat, for such was our tradition going all the way back to
ancient Spain. Many were the times in Spain when priests
carried swords under their cassocks in order to be able to
quickly take to the field against the Moors. Yes, I was a

man of peace but I was also a loyal Mexican patriot. I was very much at home with the concept of the warrior priest and I would have fought for my country if for one moment I had thought that military resistance was not hopeless.

I knew, however, that here in New Mexico we didn't even have the military means to resist the frequent attacks of the Navajos, the Apaches, and the Comanches. How were we to resist the attack of a well-organized, well-fed, and well-equipped army? For I knew that behind those boys dressed in blue were tens of thousands and hundreds of thousands more who would be sent to suppress armed resistance.

And so, I counseled another kind of resistance. I urged my people to remain faithful to their religion, to their culture, to their language. I remained with my people through a dark time. I never considered accepting the offer of the Treaty of Guadalupe Hidalgo to move south of the new border. I remained with my people through a dark time. I urged them to learn the new ways of the *americanos,* to hold on as well as they could to what was theirs, and to try to survive into a better time. Time and chance were now gambling with my people, and I remained with them as their priest of Taos.

13

Surely, I thought, time and chance had no new tricks to play on me. Don't we always think that way when we have suffered a great deal? And aren't we almost always wrong? For those two gamblers, time and chance, like to deal from the bottom of the deck. *Siempre nos sacan cartas de abajo.* And our dreams can turn to nightmares. For some *americanos,* their dreams of manifest destiny certainly became nightmares.

Not all of my fellow *nuevomexicanos* were willing to listen to calm reason. We had our share of hotheads. Trouble was brewing. Right where it always brewed in New Mexico—in Taos. There was a plot against the *americanos* in December of 1846 but it was discovered. Then, a few weeks later, in January of 1847, a terrible tragedy occurred. A mob of people in Taos attacked and killed Governor Bent, the first territorial governor appointed by the *americanos,* and the mob also killed Narciso Beaubien and Sheriff Vigil. I was on my way to church to celebrate the Mass when the mob came charging down the street. When I discovered what had happened, I lashed out at the mob and urged them to cease and desist from the folly of their ways. I harbored as many families as I could under my own roof to prevent them from being harmed by the rebels. This "Taos uprising," as it was called, ended in disaster for the rebels. There were many deaths. The leaders of the uprising were hanged by the *americanos* under the command of Colonel Sterling Price. *(He turns toward Willa)* Ah, I remember now, Willa, what it was you said about me in your novel. Words to the effect that I was responsible for the Taos uprising. Strange, isn't it, that I was elected to the Territorial Assembly *after* the Taos uprising? And strange, isn't it, that the Territorial Assembly elected me *president* of the Assembly? What do you make of that, Willa? Do you think your fellow *americanos* were so naive, so easily duped, that they would elect as President of the Territorial Assembly a man who had led a military uprising against them? *(He turns back toward the audience.) ¡Ah qué mujer!*

And so the painful episode passed. The Mexican period receded into the dream time, as the Spanish period had before, and we *nuevomexicanos* settled down to survival and to trying to understand our new conquerors. The task was difficult enough, for we had to struggle with the new language, the new school systems, the new laws, the new land and commercial regulations, all the new political, social, and economic institutions dominated, of course, by the English-speaking *americanos.*

14

It was difficult enough as it was without also having to get used to a new bishop. We *curas mexicanos,* we Mexican priests, were quite comfortable under the jurisdiction of Durango. After the change in government and the coming to power of the *americanos,* there were occasional rumors about a new diocese being created in New Mexico but we had virtually no knowledge of how Holy Mother Church administered its spiritual realm within this English-speaking nation. Indeed, there were rumors that if a new bishopric were to be created, then I might be nominated to become the new bishop. After all, I had trained many of the younger clergy, and they quite naturally championed my cause. Not that I sought the honor. The idea never occurred to me. But there were rumors to that effect and my nomination was, after all, a logical one. As I said, however, I did not seek the honor. I never gave it much thought. You can imagine the surprise of our *curas mexicanos,* then, when we learned that we were to have a new bishop, a certain don Juan Lamy, a Frenchman who was to reside in Santa Fe. Bishop Jean Baptiste Lamy. A young French priest who spoke neither Spanish nor English very well.

¿Pues que se podía hacer? I tried to make our new bishop feel welcome. *(Addressing the ghost of Bishop Lamy)* Isn't that so, Bishop Lamy? I wasn't able to go down to Santa Fe when you arrived there in August of 1851 but do you remember how splendidly we got along when you came up to Taos early the next year, in the month of March? Do you remember the good talks we had about canon law and theology? I would still like to pursue some of those questions with you. Do you remember how pleased you were with my seminary and the fine young men I was training there for the priesthood? I thought we could be such good friends but no, you wouldn't have it, would you, Bishop Lamy? You tired quickly of my interest in canon law and you let your little friend, yes, that runty little priest, Father Machebeuf, turn you away from the path of peace and cooperation with the native clergy.

(Turning alternately to the audience and to Bishop Lamy and Willa Cather, Padre Martínez is keenly aware of these two audiences)

Machebeuf! That priest couldn't respect the seal of confession. Mischief maker! He ran around carrying tales about the priests. But oh, yes, you listened to him, didn't you, Bishop Lamy? You and Machebeuf were the closest of friends, weren't you? And you, Willa, couldn't you as a novelist see beneath the surface of things? No, you only saw the close friendship between the bishop and Father Machebeuf. What is it you called Machebeuf in your novel?—oh yes, Father Vaillant, such a noble name! You obviously didn't see that that friendship could hatch a nest of vipers—lies about myself, lies about the native clergy, and a growing disillusionment on the part of the Spanish-speaking clergy with our first bishop in New Mexico under the new dispensation.

Yet there still remained time for the bishop and myself to address our differences. Had the atmosphere not been so charged with gossip and rumor, perhaps it would have all ended differently. By 1856, I was sixty-three years old. I knew that my time would soon be drawing to a close. I certainly did not wish to exit this earthly realm in an ugly atmosphere. I renewed all my efforts to remain friends with the bishop. Yes, I protested the abuse of the confessional by Father Machebeuf, but my opposition to Machebeuf was loyalty to the bishop. *(Turning toward the ghost of Bishop Lamy)* I certainly underestimated the power of friendship between two old cronies from France, didn't I, Bishop Lamy? Oh, you two were close. I never thought that my criticisms of Machebeuf, out of loyalty to you and my Church, would sour our early friendship, bishop. You certainly showed where you stood though, I'll say that much for you.

(Turning toward the audience) I wrote a letter to Bishop Lamy complaining of my infirmities brought on by old age and offering to resign my position as curate of Taos if he, the bishop, would allow me to prepare a young priest as my successor. This did not seem to be such an unreasonable request, given my advanced age and also my vast knowledge of northern New Mexico. The Bishop, however, did something that deeply saddened and outraged me. He chose to interpret my letter as a resignation. He completely ignored the condition I had attached. Instead of sending me a young priest to train as my successor, he sent me that hard-bitten Spaniard, Father Dámaso Taladrid, who proceeded to make life utterly miserable for me. He denied me the use of altar boys to assist in preparation for my daily celebration of the Mass. He stung my pride deeply by refusing to allow me to celebrate the wedding Mass of my niece. I said the Mass anyway, of course. Eventually, the bishop did remove Taladrid from my parish. *(He turns to the ghost of Bishop Lamy)* And I *still* thank you for that, Bishop Lamy. *(Turning back toward the audience)* But too much damage had already been done by gossip, stubborn pride, and maliciousness.

15

You see, there were certain issues that divided the native clergy, including myself, of course, from the bishop. There was that troublesome issue of the cathedral. When Bishop Lamy arrived in Santa Fe I hoped that he would come to love our Cathedral of Saint Francis. The old adobe cathedral. Bishop Lamy took one look at it and he called it a "mud-pie palace." He didn't like adobe. He wanted to construct a new cathedral in the romanesque style such as he had become accustomed to in Lempdes, in southern France. The problem was, Where was the money supposed to come from? With the American separation of church and state, there wasn't any hope of financing the rebuilding project there. The money was finally supposed to come from where it always comes from in New Mexico, from the poorest people who can least afford to pay. So Bishop Lamy issued his famous Circular to the Clergy of 1854, imposing a new tithe, under *pain of excommunication* for those who would not comply with the tithe. We priests were no longer to baptize our infants without first imposing the new tithe. We priests were no longer to marry our youngsters in Holy Mother Church without first imposing the new tithe. We priests were no longer to bury our dead in the *camposanto,* the holy ground, unless we first collected the new tithe. I studied the Circular very carefully. And I realized that Bishop Lamy simply didn't understand the barter nature of society in New Mexico. So I ignored the Circular. And I continued to baptize our infants, and marry our youngsters, and bury our dead in the *camposanto,* and I continued to collect eggs and chickens, small sacks of beans and corn, goat meat and deer hides, and other such items in lieu of cash, for you see there was very little money in New Mexico. And I thought, surely sooner or later Bishop Lamy will see the error of his Circular and withdraw it.

Then there was the matter of the beautiful art of our *santeros,* our woodcarvers who crafted *bultos,* carvings in the round, and *retablos,* flat pieces, to decorate our churches. Our *santeros* had very few models for their work. Perhaps an occasional illustration in a Bible, or a rare painting of a sacred theme that made its way here from Spain or Mexico. But for the most part our *santeros* had to rely on their faith and their imagination to carve their images for the churches. The early *santeros* worked in the tradition of holy men, and their work remains anonymous, for they refused to sign their names to work that was meant to honor God and not to honor themselves as artists. Well, Bishop Lamy had no use for the wood carvings. He saw them as some kind of evil, mean-spirited bloody things, and he tried to have as many of them destroyed as he possibly could. Bishop Lamy almost succeeded in destroying the art of the New Mexican *santero.* Oh, he replaced the carvings, of course. He replaced them with cheap lithographs that came down the Santa Fe Trail and later, so I have learned, with plaster-of-paris statues, those bulky, ugly things that some wit referred to as "bathrobe art."

Most troublesome of all, there was the question of La Santa Hermandad de Nuestro Padre Jesús, the Holy Brotherhood of Our Lord Jesus Christ, better known to you, perhaps, as los Penitentes, the Penitente Brotherhood, because of acts of penance the brotherhood would perform during Holy Week. Here in New Mexico, where we had so few priests, the brotherhood performed many good social deeds and helped to preserve the religious tone of the far-flung villages. The last Franciscan priest in the territory had given me permission to be the spiritual advisor of the Third Order of Saint Francis and so I assisted the brothers who, in my opinion, much resembled the Third Order, as best I could to help them organize their *moradas,* or religious meeting places. Bishop Lamy, with his fresh and entirely negative memories of the French Revolution, viewed the Penitentes as a threat to his authority, as some kind of a state within a state, and he proceeded to suppress them. Well, what could I do? I was their spiritual advisor. So I continued to assist them in strengthening their organization so that they would be able to deal with the new conditions created by the coming to power of the United States in this territory.

Despite my efforts to retain the friendship of the bishop, it seemed that our differences, and perhaps also our poor communications, fed one upon the other and matters went from bad to worse. Anyway, the bishop sent that runty friend of his, Machebeuf, to Taos to "whip the cats," as he used to say, in order to read my excommunication. I urged my people to listen respectfully to Father Machebeuf, and so the faithful sat in silence as he fulminated against me. Some of the *americanos,* landgrabbers and opportunists who hated me, men like Kit Carson, Charles Beaubien, and Ceran St. Vrain, tried to spark rumors of violence, but I was always a peaceful man. At times I was headstrong, yes, but at heart I was a peaceful man.

16

What did I think about the excommunication? I didn't like it. And I didn't believe in it. The bishop had ignored the procedures of Canon Law. Why, the more I thought about the excommunication, the more I realized it wasn't worth the piece of paper it was written on. I knew that since I was an ecclesiastical attorney, something I have failed to mention so far, that I would be able to crush the excommunication were I a younger man and physically capable of making the long and arduous journey to Rome. The bishop knew he was on slippery ground. *(Turning to Bishop Lamy)* Isn't that so, bishop? *(Turning back to audience)* And he knew that I knew it. So he left me alone. He ignored me. Pretended I didn't exist. But he very wisely did not attempt to remove me from my Church. So I ignored the excommunication. And I continued to accept payment for religious services in goats and chickens, and in *ristras* of chile. And I continued to minister to the needs of my faithful *nuevomexicanos.*

(Turning to Bishop Lamy) You probably thought I didn't have much longer to live after the excommunication. Isn't that so? But I fooled you! *(Turning to audience)* And I fooled myself. I seemed to have a new burst of energy for awhile. Even my interest in politics revived. But for the most part, I ministered to the needs of my people. That wasn't as easy for an old man as you might think.

One night I heard shouting and screaming. The cry of a woman in distress. The sounds came closer and suddenly there was a loud pounding on my front door and then the door burst open. It was Juan Sánchez and his wife María. He had a wild look about him and his eyes were huge and crazy. He had his belt fastened around her neck and she was absolutely terrified. It was she who had pounded and clawed at my door and now, half-dead with fear and with the very air being choked out of her body, she fell to her knees *(Padre Martínez demonstrates)* and screamed "Padre, *¡socorro! ¡sálvame!*" "Help, save me!," she screamed.

"What happened?" I asked. "And take that belt off her neck!"

"I caught her whoring!" That's what Juan Sánchez said to me.

"And now you want to be the hangman?" I roared at him. "Get that belt off her neck."

He slowly loosened his grip and the belt fell away. Then he began to cry.

"And you," I said to her, "is it true? Were you whoring around?"

"Yes, padre. It is true. I'm sorry," she said. And she broke down and started crying.

Well, with all this crying, I felt like crying, too. And I grabbed both of them and shook them hard. Then I turned to Juan Sánchez and I said to him, "didn't I see you just yesterday stumbling out of the *cantina* slurping a bottle of wine?"

"Sí, padre," he said.

"Well, that bottle is your whore," I rebuked him. "If you didn't spend so much time with your whore maybe you would have more time to spend with your wife."

"And you," I said to María, "what were you doing sleeping around?"

"I don't know, padre," she said. And she cried all the more.

What could I do? I was on the verge of rebuking her most severely when I remembered the story of Jesus and the woman taken in adultery. The Pharisees brought a woman taken in adultery to Jesus and he refused to condemn her. He gathered together a little mound of stones. "He that is without sin among you, let him first cast a stone," Jesus had said. One by one, the Pharisees walked away.

I could not cast the first stone. I remembered all the times in my life when I felt cheated. I remembered when I had lost my lovely young wife so many years ago at the moment of childbirth. And I could not cast the first stone. I remembered the sudden death of my daughter. And I could not cast the first stone. I remembered the empty feeling inside me when I received word that the United States had invaded us. And I could not cast the first stone. I remembered the new bishop coming to Santa Fe and all my hopes for my ecclesiastical career vanishing. And I could not cast the first stone. Now these two suffering people stood before me, both sinners as I was a sinner, and all three of us hurting with the inevitable hurt of living. And I could not cast the first stone. I embraced them both. I told them the story of Jesus and the woman taken in adultery. And oh, I looked Juan Sánchez right in the eye, for I knew he had slept with more than just his wife or a bottle of wine. He dropped his eyes and said nothing. And I told María she would be happier if she spent less time at the *cantina* and more time reading and learning and helping me in my old age to educate her children. They thanked me and they left silently.

Did they ever have problems again? I don't know, but they probably did. Isn't that very human? I hope that their future brought them the good dreams they certainly wanted and that the bad dreams, or nightmares, remained few and far between, if they occurred at all. After they left, I sat for a long time in my living room. Suddenly, I felt my age and I grew weary. It had been too much excitement for an old priest. I had seen too much suffering in my time.

And I knew the bishop was suffering. He couldn't enjoy the state of affairs between us any more than I could. But he was much younger than me and I knew that time and chance would soon relieve him of the burden I was to him. I remembered that had my daughter lived, she would have been one year younger than this young French bishop. But time and chance bring us all to a state where human time and human chance cease to exist. We have this saying in Spanish: *En cien años todos seremos calvos.* In a hundred years we will all be bald.

17

The very next day, I gathered together my papers and prepared my will. I divided up my few possessions among my many kinsmen. I didn't forget those orphans to whom I had given the name Martínez. *(He turns to the ghost of Willa*

Cather.) These were my "children," Willa. It's a pity you didn't see fit to write about them. I understand, of course, that a novel has its own truth. As does history, Willa. If only you had been a little more charitable with me. Then again, you might also be suffering like the good bishop. If you had lived but a few decades earlier perhaps we might have met and you might have had a different opinion of me. After all, we are all children, orphans in exile in this world, in this earthly dream where we prepare for a greater dream time to come.

(Turning back to the audience) Even in this dream time there are people who care for orphans. And so I also set a few things aside for doña Teodora. As a reward for her many years of service to the Church, and to me, and . . . but I don't want to give rise to scandal. No, no, I won't go into this question in any detail. There might be another Willa lurking nearby. Just let me say that she was a good and kindly woman and I rewarded her for her merits.

With my earthly possessions accounted for, I then chose my own epitaph. It was a quotation from the Old Testament, from the Book of Ecclesiastes, chapter 9, verse 11:

> *Volví*
> *Y vi bajo el sol*
> *Que la carrera no es de los ligeros*
> *Ni la batalla de los fuertes . . .*
> *Mas el tiempo y la suerte*
> *Les ocurre a todos.*

> I returned
> And saw under the sun

That the race is not to the swift
Nor the battle to the strong . . .
But time and chance happeneth to them all.

Time and chance, those two old gamblers, had taken so much from me. But they had also given me the opportunity to reflect on my life and times. They taught me the humility to see that we are never as much in control of our destiny as we would like to think. Not I. Not you. Not even Willa or the Bishop.

All we can do is work and play together. And oftentimes cry. And dream. We can try to share our good dreams and make our nightmares less painful. For if time and chance have taught me anything at all, it is that we must try to heal these wounds that we inflict upon one another. Maybe that's the clue to this cosmic mystery we wander in. We move along in this celestial voyage and time and time again, we have the chance to heal our wounds, to help one another. Maybe time and chance, those two ancient gamblers, are working for someone who knows all the odds. *(He laughs to himself.)* Maybe God does play dice.

Ah, but I'm beginning to sound like a preacher. And I really must be on my way. Someday, somewhere, soon, on my celestial voyage, I hope to encounter the bishop. *(He looks over his shoulder.)* He might even be lurking nearby. He and I have no quarrel over Church dogma and theology. But I would like to discuss certain matters of Canon Law with him. There are some issues there that he and I have yet to settle. And someday soon, I trust I shall encounter Willa. I would like to discuss with her in great detail the theory of fiction as opposed to the theory of history. *(He looks over his shoulder again.)* She's probably scribbling away out there. I can hardly wait to speak to her. And now, I really must be going, *mis hijos,* my children, for the voyage is long and I have scarcely begun my travels. I trust we will also meet again soon and we can resume our discussions of these weighty matters. Remember to travel lightly. I now travel as light as a shadow, as light as the traces I leave of myself in your minds, in your dreams. *Adiós.*

THE END

VOLVÍ
Y VI
BAJO EL SOL

PADRE MARTÍNEZ DE TAOS

Personaje:
Padre Antonio José Martínez, el Cura de Taos

El Decorado:
Este drama le da al Padre Martínez la oportunidad de volver de donde descansa en paz para responder a las acusaciones que la historia y las circunstancias le han dirigido. Específicamente, Padre Martínez quiere responder a los espectros históricos del Arzobispo Jean Baptiste Lamy, el primer obispo, y más tarde arzobispo, de Santa Fe después de la llegada del poder político de Estados Unidos al suroeste, y Willa Cather, escritora célebre que criticó al Padre Martínez de una manera bastante cruel en su novela, La Muerte Viene Por El Arzobispo.
Lo que se pone en la escena es mínimo para dejar lugar a un máximo de flexibilidad y un mínimo de costo en hacer la representación como drama que pudiera viajar en camino de teatro en teatro. El número de escenas es también flexible para dejar lugar a representaciones cortas con una preparación apropiada (véase la Introducción) igual que una producción entera.
Vestido en sotana de cura de iglesia, o algo semejante, el

63

personaje sale bajo un reflector cerca del centro de la escena. El personaje puede entrar o de la izquierda o de la derecha. Alejado un poco del centro, al lado izquierdo, está una silla, el único apoyo en la escena. Si hay iluminación en el teatro, una decoración en el foro con reflectores de un suave color rojo bajo puede proveer un ambiente bueno para el drama. El Padre Martínez hará su papel hacia el proscenio y utilizará la silla como indicado en las direcciones de la escena o como quisiera el director modificarlas.

I

Entra el PADRE MARTÍNEZ. *Es viejo, doblado, y se ve ensimismado. Anda despacio hacia el centro de la escena, cruza por enfrente de la silla y entonces regresa y se sienta, mirando hacia el público.*

PADRE MARTÍNEZ *(santiguándose o con las manos en postura de oración; se despierta como de una meditación profunda):*

> *¿Qué es la vida?, un frenesí;*
> *¿Qué es la vida?, una ilusión,*
> *Una sombra, una ficción,*
> *Y el mayor bien es pequeño;*
> *Que toda la vida es sueño*
> *Y los sueños, sueños son.*

Palabras del gran poeta y dramaturgo, Calderón de la Barca. Sí, sí entiendo que debiera usar el idioma de la nueva

ley, el inglés. Estas palabras que vengo murmurando son
de un gran poeta y dramaturgo, Calderón de la Barca.

¿Qué es la vida?, pregunta. Un frenesí. Una ilusión. Una
sombra, una ficción. Y el mayor bien, todo lo que llevamos
a cabo en esta vida, es poco porque la vida es sueño. Y los
sueños sueños son.

Ahora vuelvo de los sueños para compartir con Uds. mis
ambiciones, mis victorias, las derrotas, y los sueños. Vamos
de un sueño a otro en este viaje celestial. Somos ambiciosos
y nuestras ambiciones tienen éxito o se vuelven cenizas.
Tenemos nuestras victorias. Y hasta las victorias se vuelven
derrotas. Y en medio de un fracaso nos agarramos a una
victoria inesperada. Se acaba un sueño y otro comienza. Vamos de sueño en sueño buscando la luz que nos alumbrará
en nuestro viaje a otro sueño. Y el tiempo y la esperanza
son los jugadores que apuestan con nuestro sino que va de
sueño en sueño. Estos jugadores siempre nos sacan cartas
de abajo, o así nos parece a nosotros a quienes no se nos
ha dado el don de saber cuáles son las fuerzas de la luz y de
las tinieblas que guían a estos jugadores celestiales. Mas nos
basta nuestra fe para mantenernos firmes en los momentos
más pésimos.

2

*(Se levanta de la silla, poniéndose de pie, y mira hacia el fondo
y a la derecha. Hace esto para indicar que habla con los espectros invisibles del Arzobispo Lamy y de Willa Cather.)*

Sé que me están escuchando allá en lo alto, en las nieblas. ¡Ah qué gente! Esa mujer. ¿Cómo se llamaba? Willa. Sí, Willa. La señora Willa Cather. ¡Y el buen obispo! Ojalá que me encuentre con ellos pronto. Hay tantas cosas que quisiera discutir con ellos. ¡Ay, qué mujer! ¡Qué cosas tan horribles me echó en cara en esa novela que escribió! Sí, esa novela *La Muerte Viene Por El Arzobispo*.

(Camina para arriba y abajo, refuñuñando entre los dientes cuando no se dirige al público.)

Ella dijo que yo tenía los colmillos largos y amarillentos. Dijo que yo era lujurioso y que codiciaba a las mujeres. Bueno, pues, ¿acaso han conocido a un hombre a quien no le gustan las mujeres? Y, ¿qué más dijo? Sí, dijo que yo tenía tantos hijos, ¡Qué lástima que no me conoció como un hombre de carne y hueso! Quizás me hubiera encontrado menos pintoresco . . . y menos pícaro.

Sí, lástima también que la señora Cather no lo conoció al buen obispo. Quizás le hubiera encontrado menos santucho como lo dibujó en esa novela suya. Por lo contrario, era defendor militante de la iglesia por su propia cuenta pero tan obstinado y con una falta pasmosa de comprensión de los nuevomexicanos.

¿Me oyes, señor obispo? Dije *falta de comprensión*. De allí no sale ud. del paso. Y Ud., señora Cather, ¿qué sabía Ud. de mis hijos?

3

(Dirigiéndose hacia el público) Oh, no se me han olvidado los hijos. Sé que ese tema les interesa muchísimo. *(Se sienta en la silla.)* Pues, voy a contarles de mis hijos. Hubo muchos.

Cuando pienso en mis hijos, todavía los puedo ver sentados en los bancos rudos que yo tenía como sillas dentro de la escuela, el seminario de la Virgen de Guadalupe que yo dirigía en Taos . . . en la sala de mi propia casa.

(Se levanta y camina un poco hacia la derecha y de vez en cuando se dirige hacia un lugar a la derecha del escenario que es su "escuela." El director tiene toda libertad en dirigir esto en la escena.)

Vigilaba a mis hijos cuando estudiaban. Los enseñaba en su lengua natal, por supuesto, el español, y les enseñaba el catecismo, la ortografía, la aritmética, todo que yo pensaba que les podría ayudar en un mundo que estaba cambiando rápidamente. También les enseñaba el inglés. Por si acaso. Por si acaso ese gigante del norte tan amistoso, los Estados Unidos, se decidiera a hacerse menos amistoso.

También les enseñaba a mis hijos algo de la ley. Debieran saber que nosotros, los nuevomexicanos que hablamos español, nosotros los españoles y mestizos, ya que la mayoría teníamos sangre india, solíamos decir ese hombre *es hombre de su palabra.* Sabía yo, sin embargo, que bajo la ley norteamericana lo que quedaba escrito en papel era de mayor importancia. Por esta razón, les enseñaba a mis hijos todo lo que sabía yo de la ley americana. Yo les decía: *la nación americana es un burro en que van montado los abogados.* ¿Saben Uds. lo que es lidiar con los abogados? Pues, a mí no me gustaba tratar con ellos y por esto me hice abogado—de la iglesia por supuesto. *(Mirando hacia atrás)* ¿Verdad que fue así mi ilustrísimo señor obispo? ¿Es ésta la razón por qué Ud. tenía tanto miedo de enfrentarse conmigo? ¿Sospechaba Ud. la debilidad del pleito que tenía conmigo? ¡Qué gran ventaja para Ud. que ya estaba yo viejo y enfermo cuando hubo esa bronca entre nosotros! De otra manera, con los conocimientos de la ley eclesiástica que yo tenía . . . pues, ¿quién sabe como hubieran resultado las cosas? *(Dirigiéndose hacia el público.)* Hice todo lo posible, en fin, para preparar a mis hijos para los cambios inevitables que venían. Oh, ¡el orgullo que sentía al ver mis hijos! Trabajé tanto tratando de educarlos lo mismo que esta noche trato de educarlos a Uds. *(Dirigido al público)* ¿Uds. son mis hijos! Igual que lo eran mis estudiantes en ese Taos ya desaparecido del siglo pasado. ¿Cómo pudiera Willa Cather haberme acusado de ser el padre carnal de mis propios estudiantes? ¿Y tanto que me echó en cara! Ay, ¡qué mujer! *(Dirigiéndose hacia el fondo a la derecha, hacia Willa Cather.)* Ud. tiene cierta culpabilidad en este caso, señora. Ud. no pensaba en mis "hijos" como si esa palabrita no indicara que eran mis estudiantes, ¿verdad? ¿Era tan importante para esa novela apoyar uno de los cargos más desacreditados que se pueden hacer contra un cura, contra cualquier cura? ¡Qué mujer! Algún día, señora Cather, tenemos que juntarnos y hablar de estos asuntos.

4

(Se dirige hacia el público.) Oh, no quiero que me entiendan mal. No voy a ponerme de pie aquí ante uds. en este momento del proceso y aparentar gozar de virtudes que no son mías. No nací para hacerme cura de la iglesia. ¡Sépanlo bien! Cuando yo nací en Abiquiu en 1793 y entonces nos mudamos a Taos en 1804, mis padres don Antonio Severino Martínez y mi madre doña María del Carmen Santisteban, y yo, pues no me criaron para ser cura. Nací para hacerme vaquero. Lo que se llama un *cowboy* en inglés, un ranchero al estilo norteño.

Pues cuando yo era del tamaño de un saltamontes, podía cabalgar así como cualquier vaquero norteño. Jugábamos este juego. Un juego que nuestros antepasados les habían enseñado a los indios del pueblo de San Juan. El juego se llamaba *el gallo.* Cogíamos a un gallo y lo enterrábamos hasta el pescuezo en la arena. Entonces a caballo formábamos una media luna alrededor del gallo, y a todo galope tratábamos de ver quien podía precipitarse de la silla y agarrar al gallo desdichado por el pescuezo y sacarlo de la arena de un jalón. Al gallo no le gustaba. Juego bastante duro y cruel, Uds. dirán. Sí, pero esos eran tiempos duros y a veces crueles en la frontera de Taos a los principios del siglo diecinueve.

Así gocé de los años de mi juventud. Aprendí todos los oficios de un vaquero, un ranchero, porque como el primer hijo, yo sabía que algún día sería heredor del rancho de mi padre y de todas sus posesiones y tendría que hacerme buen mayordomo de lo que sería entregado a mi cuidado. Me gustaba la riata y el cabalgar, y el marcar con hierro a las vacas. Imposible olvidarme de la vista de la llegada de las caravanas de mi padre después de haber cumplido el viaje tan arduo desde la Ciudad de México y de Chihuahua. Las carretas llegaban llenas pero rellenas de todo lo que nos hacía falta en la frontera—clavos de fierro, lujo raro en la frontera, fierros de mano, platos, especias muy raras, objetos de plata, cuero fino, y tantas cosas que nos faltaban, y los muy pocos lujos que podíamos permitirnos en este país donde casi no existía el dinero.

5

Pues así fue mi juventud. Un día se me acercó mi padre, don Antonio Severino, y traía consigo a una joven. Cuando vi cómo sus trenzas negras se caían como una cascada sobre su hombro y su pecho, pues todo eso me atraía. Nos hicimos muy amigos. Por las tardes dábanos paseos largos bajo el cielo brillante de Taos. Como todos los amantes, pensábamos que el cielo nos pertenecía sólo a nosotros. Sí, y así pensaban los amantes que vivieron antes de nosotros y muy antes de esos pintores que más tarde dieron a conocer a Taos con sus montes y cielos a todo el mundo. Fue como si una luz nueva hubiera entrado en mi vida. De veras, así se llamaba ella. María de la Luz. Pronto nos casamos. Sí, sí fue un casorio arreglado, por cierto, porque esa era nuestra costumbre. Pero aunque hubiera sido arreglado, el matrimonio resultó a lo menos tan feliz como los matrimonios de los tiempos modernos que nadie los arregla y que se acaban a veces muy pronto.

Por todo un año demasiado breve, gocé de toda la felicidad del matrimonio. Al cabo de ese año, ya se le llegó su hora a María de la Luz de dar a luz a una criatura. En aquel entonces no teníamos la medicina moderna de que Uds. gozan y en el momento de dar a luz pues perdimos a mi mujer. Hicimos todo lo posible para salvar la vida de nuestra niña y a lo menos conseguimos eso, gracias a Dios. En recuerdo de su madre le llamamos y nombramos María de la Luz.

Dolorido en mi alma por haber perdido tanto, comencé a leer la Santa Biblia buscando consuelo. Entre más leía los sagrados textos, más me ponía a pensar si de veras tenía yo vocación de cura de la iglesia. Le escribí al obispo en Durango. El me respondió. La correspondencia duró cuatro años y el obispo insistió en que me fuera al sur, en que dejara a mi familia y entrara en el seminario para ver si de veras tenía vocación de sacerdote.

6

(El Padre Martínez camina hacia la extrema derecha del escenario y con despacio vuelve hacia el centro durante el monólogo siguiente.)

Todavía es invierno durante los meses de febrero y marzo en Taos, ¿saben Uds.? Y era durante esa época, en un tal día tan frío, el año de 1817 que me despedí de don Antonio Severino y doña María del Carmen Santistéban y también de mi hija, María de la Luz que ya comenzaba a madurar como una flor. Era momento triste y lleno de ternura cuando nos abrazamos mi papá, mi mamá, mi hija y yo. Sabía que no los vería por muchos largos años. Pero el aire estaba fresco esa mañana y yo sabía que los años que venían serían años de aventura y de educación. Años de aventura para este joven nuevomexicano que había oído tantos cuentos de México contados por los flecheros de las carretas que trabajaban para mi padre en sus negocios de comerciante en el camino de Chihuahua que corría desde Chihuahua a Taos.

Y así me despedí de Taos. Seguí el curso del río sagrado, el río bravo, o el río del norte que hoy día se llama el Río Grande, hacia el sur, hacia Santa Fe, la ciudad de nuestra fe santa, y luego pasé por Alburquerque. Siguiendo la pista, pasé por Belén, el pueblo del santo niño Jesús, y después por Socorro. ¿Verdad que muchas veces necesitamos socorro en la vida? Cabalgué más al sur pasando por San Antonio y luego por una aldea que nosotros llamábamos Las Palomas. Nombre bonito, ¿verdad? Después, bajo los americanos, cambiaron el nombre a Hot Springs, que todavía suena bien. Me he dado cuenta que muchos años después de mi muerte hubo una nueva invención, algo eléctrico, la radio, y hubo entonces un programa de radio y no sé qué, y la gente del pueblo cambió el nombre de la aldea a Truth or Consequences, o sea, La Verdad o las Consecuencias.

(Mueve la cabeza expresando su incredulidad.) Siempre fui liberal en el sentido clásico del liberalismo del siglo diez y nueve. Siempre fui partidario del cambio, del progreso. Pero ocurren cosas que le hacen a uno pensar. Seguí mi rumbo hacia el sur, pasando por la jornada del muerto, y entonces a El Paso del Norte. No existía entonces, claro, Ciudad Juárez. Montado a caballo, pasé por Chihuahua hasta llegar a Durango.

7

Si Uds. pudieran haber visto a México en aquellos tiempos. Era la época del movimiento para la independencia. México se alzaba contra el gachupín, el español que se había apoderado del país. Pues me inscribí en el seminario y comencé los estudios de teología y de metafísica. Tengo que admitir que me costó mucho a veces poner la atención en los libros y los estudios cuando la política hervía por todos lados.

Por todo México, en las grandes ciudades, se oían los lemas de la revolución francesa: ¡Libertad, Justicia, Igualdad! Todo era tan emocionante. Todavía era yo joven y pensába que vivía en el crepúsculo de la libertad. Los Estados Unidos al norte ya habían establecido la unión democrática liberal y ahora parecía que México estaba para levantar vela en un viaje semejante. Qué lástima que aprendiera yo muy pronto que tras de esos lemas, esas palabras tan emocionantes de la revolución, venía la sangre.

Quisiera que Uds. se recordaran sin embargo que

aprendí la política no por la lectura ni por los discursos de
los políticos, sino por las palabras recordadas del gran jefe
del movimiento de independencia, el Padre Miguel Hidalgo.
Sí, aprendí de las palabras de un gran cura, el Padre Miguel
Hidalgo, que un cura puede cuidar del bienestar de su rebaño, de sus parroquianos, de sus *hijos,* aquí en este mundo
tanto como del bienestar en el reinado que viene después
de la muerte.

Así me resultó un poco difícil prestar atención a mis estudios bajo estas circunstancias tan animadas. Estudié lo
bastante, sin embargo, para graduarme con distinción y
aunque esta tos que parece haberme perseguido más allá de
la muerte siempre me molestó, todavía me quedaba bastante vida para gozar de las celebraciones de la independencia que México ganó de España en 1821. La tos empeoró,
no obstante, y mis superiores en el seminario temían que
muy pronto se me acabara la vida. Como acabo de decir
hace un rato, no teníamos la medicina de la cual Uds. gozan
hoy. Decidieron los superiores ordenarme entonces en el
año 1822, un poco antes de que cumpliera treinta años. Ya
que había recibido distinción académica y visto que mi
salud dejaba mucho que desear, me otorgaron una exención
de mi último año de estudio y me ordenaron cura un año
antes de cumplir mis estudios formales.

8

Cuando volví al norte, montado a caballo, puse atención en los pueblos tan áridos y llenos de polvo que se encontraban por todas partes en las provincias norteñas mexicanas. Por dondequiera había pobreza. Por todas partes se encontraba la fe fuerte y un amor cariñoso y feroz a la vida. Y en todas partes el tiempo y la suerte, esos grandes jugadores y árbitros de nuestro destino habían sacado cartas de abajo con la gente, con los pobres, y éstos, sin embargo, se mantenían fiel a su modo de ser, a su tierra, y a sus esperanzas de una vida mejor en esta tierra tan bella y tan áspera. Se mantenían fiel a sus sueños en este país desierto donde los sueños forman parte del paisaje.

Al llegar a Taos, allí me esperaban mis padres y también mi hija, María de la Luz, ya una doncella de once años. Como se puede imaginar, era todo esto inolvidable para mi. Comencé mi vocación de cura. Bautizaba a los niños poco después de que nacieran. Unía en matrimonio a los jóvenes cuando llegaba esa hora. Y también enterraba a nuestros difuntos en el camposanto cuando se les llegaba su hora como se nos llega a todos.

Eran tiempo que me daban mucho gusto. Los deberes de la iglesia me mantenían muy ocupado pero todavía me quedaba tiempo para pasar unos ratos con mi hija tan joven y bella. Me llenaba de alegría cada momento que montaba mi caballo más ligero y cruzaba los llanos Taoseños hasta llegar a Ranchitos donde mis padres, es decir, los abuelos, criaban a María de la Luz en su rancho. Así corrió el tiempo en ese año tan lleno de felicidad.

Pronto, demasiado pronto, este momento de sueño ideal se marchó al reinado de los sueños. Era el año 1824, y una de esas fiebres terribles se precipitó por la región. Como ya decía, nos faltaba la medicina que Uds. de la época moderna dan por supuesto. Una noche llegó un heraldo negro del rancho de mi padre.

—Véngase padre,—me dijo,—es su hija. Está malamente enferma.—

Monté a mi caballo más veloz y crucé el llano a todo galope. Llegué demasiado tarde. Tenía doce años cuando se murió.

9

¿Pues qué se podía hacer? *(Camina nerviosamente de un lado al otro por el proscenio durante esta escena. Su manera de hablar en esta escena es más rápida que de costumbre.)* Seguí siendo el buen cura de Taos. Seguí bautizando a los niños, casando a los jóvenes, y enterrando a nuestros difuntos en el campo santo. Compré una prensa de mano de ese hombre Ramón Abreu que vivía en Santa Fe. Traje la prensa y también al impresor Jesús María Baca, a Taos y comencé a publicar textos religiosos, libros de ortografía y aritmética. Publiqué volantes en donde podía dirigirme a los intereses políticos de los pobres y de los oprimidos. Abrí mi escuela, el Seminario de Nuestra Señora de Guadalupe, para muchachos y muchachas, en mi propia casa y empecé a educar a nuestros hijos e hijas. Me metí en la política. Tres veces fui candidato por la Asamblea del Departamento Mexicano. Tres veces me nombraron delegato. Con la aprobación del Obispo Zubiría en Durango, desarrollé la educación de los jóvenes para que se prepararan para el sacerdocio. De mi propia bolsa pagué los costos de los estudiantes que no tenían fondos propios para asistir a la escuela. Hice todo lo posible, en fin, para tratar de llenar esas horas tan largas y desoladas que me quedaron después de haber perdido a mi esposa y a mi hija. Y aún los días y las noches se me hacían largos y desolados, y los inviernos fríos y miserables.

Hubiera sido todavía más terrible si no hubiera sido por doña Teodora Romero, que cuidaba de mi casa. Barría y limpiaba la iglesia. Preparaba la comida y me planchaba las sotanas. Su buen sentido de humor siempre me animaba. Pero, ah, ¡no quiero causar escándalo! (*Mirando hacia atrás se dirige a Willa Cather allá en la oscuridad del fondo a la derecha de la escena.*) Ud. ve esto de doña Teodora con vista maligna, ¿verdad, señora Cather? Qué lástima que le gustaba tanto el escándalo en esa novela. Tendremos que discutir este asunto, señora. (*Dirigiéndose al público.*) ¡Qué mujer! De todos modos, doña Teodora era buena mujer y además ... pero no, no quiero causar escándalo. Permítanme tan siquiera decir que ella sirvió bien a la iglesia y asistió a este humilde cura en sus quehaceres.

El tiempo y la suerte me trajeron nuevos peligros, nuevas oportunidades. El gobierno mexicano me nombró cónsul para los americanos que llegaban a Taos porque yo sabía bien el inglés. Vigilé con mucha atención la llegada constante de tantos americanos. Yo sabía que el gobierno mexicano se había equivocado en permitir pasar americanos por

el camino de Santa Fe que se abrió en 1821. Como muchos
habían hecho, traté de avisar a mi gobierno que nuestras
fronteras se extendían demasiado y que los americanos estaban entrando a nuestro querido México por toda la frontera norteña. Por supuesto, yo me opuse a los esfuerzos de
los ricos americanos de adquirir grandes concesiones de terrenos por medio de la formación de sociedades anónimas en
nombre colectivo con mexicanos que o no sospechaban nada
o eran codiciosos. México, que se desesperaba para obtener
ingresos consintió en esas donaciones trágicas de tierras
que prepararon el camino para la invasión norteamericana.

10

Pasaron los años. Llegó el año 1837 y el gobierno mexicano, que siempre trataba de aumentar los ingresos, impuso
nuevos impuestos en los territorios norteños. Yo me opuse
a los nuevos impuestos porque me daba cuenta de la pobreza de nuestra gente. Entendía y simpatizaba, por supuesto, con los aprietos del gobierno mexicano. Torturado
por las guerras civiles en el Yucatán y en Tejas (aunque no
sé por qué alguien quisiera tomar posesión de Tejas), la
joven República Mexicana necesitaba dinero para reclutar
las tropas que se suponía acabarían con los varios movimientos separatistas. Simpatizaba con México, sí, pero yo
sabía que ni con impuestos habría suficiente dinero en todo
Nuevo México para ayudar al gobierno: ¿Saben Uds. lo difícil que es ganar dinero en Nuevo México? Como ya dije,

me opuse a los nuevos impuestos y mandé una carta a *La Gaceta,* ese periódico en Santa Fe, protestando tales impuestos.

Las palabras mías animaron algo que no me había propuesto. Pronto los campesinos y los rancheros del valle de Santa Cruz, los de Chimayó, rehusaron pagar los impuestos y se alzaron en rebelión contra el gobierno mexicano. Y aunque fuera débil, el gobierno mexicano todavía tenía suficiente fuerza para mandar sus dragones a la frontera norteña. Fue una guerra breve, tragicómica, y trágica a la vez como todas las guerras. Los rebeldes avanzaron a Santa Fe, tomaron la capital, y mataron al gobernador, Albino Pérez. Y muy pronto en 1838, las tropas mexicanas bajo el mando de ese joven advenedizo de Alburquerque, Manuel Armijo, echaron a los rebeldes de Santa Fe. Algunos fueron executados. Otros huyeron a sus aldeas y pueblos.

Triste y harto de la matanza, volví a mi parroquia de Taos y no quise tener nada que ver jamás con la política. Para hombre de mi constitución, sin embargo, era difícil mantenerme fuera de la política. Pues de un lado había este problema con los tejanos. Bajo el pretexto de tener relaciones comerciales con nosotros, lo cierto es que invadieron Nuevo México en 1841 y en 1843. Les dimos una buena lección y los echamos derrotados a Tejas. Esos tejanos nunca me engañaron. Yo veía que su "República de Tejas" era mero pretexto para que Estados Unidos nos invadiera y ocupara nuestros terrenos. Traté lo más posible de despertar a la gente para que hiciera algo para echar a los invadores y protegerse ellos a sí mismos.

Para decir la verdad, no eran los tejanos lo que yo temía,

aunque fueran rudos y enemigos de los nuevomexicanos. No, no eran tanto los tejanos como ese gigante furtivo al norte que dio luz a Tejas y luego luego se lo tragó. Sí, ese gigante que se llamaba los Estados Unidos.

II

(Mira hacia el fondo y a la derecha de la escena para dirigirse al Obispo Lamy.) Y Ud., muy señor mío, ¿cómo consideraba Ud. a los Estados Unidos? Ya había viajado desde Francia para encontrarse lejos de esos movimientos liberales democráticos y revolucionarios de Europa que tanto odiaba Ud. Ni tampoco le gustaba a Ud. la revolución francesa. Sé que había visto que la revolución destruyó mucho del poder social y político de la iglesia. Muchacho campesino, que es lo que había sido Ud. en el sur campesino de Francia, le criaron a Ud. como político conservador. Lo mismo era con la mayoría de los curas en esos tiempos. Entonces llegó Ud. a Nuevo México con todo el peso de su conservatismo a cuestas. Me extraña ¿que pudiera Ud. haber pensado de esa democracia liberal del norte, los Estados Unidos? ¿De veras admiraba Ud. tanto a Estados Unidos o era simplemente que Ud. notaba el contraste de la fuerza política y militar de ese país con la falta de tal poder en México? *(con tristeza)* Yo sé la mala opinión que tenía Ud. de nuestros nuevomexicanos.

(Se dirige de nuevo al público.) Mis sentimientos hacia Estados Unidos eran una mezcla compleja. Admiraba su con-

stitución, su separación del estado y la iglesia, sus elecciones democráticas y, en general, su gran fuente de la filosofía liberal de la cual nacieron los Estados Unidos. Realmente me daba tanto gusto ver que mi querido México creaba sus instituciones usando el patrón de Estados Unidos.

(Camina nerviosamente arriba y abajo. De vez en cuando se sienta en la silla por unos momentos.)

Claro, había cosas que no me gustaban de los Estados Unidos. No aguantaba la codicia que tenían para aumentar sus terrenos. Por eso me oponía a todos sus esfuerzos de apoderarse de nuestra tierra. Con razón no me quería el coronel Bent. Tampoco Carlos Beaubien o su hijo Narciso. Tampoco Kit Carson. Estos me veían como obstáculo a sus intereses comerciales—y tenían razón porque nunca traté de ocultar que yo me oponía a esos intereses porque iban contra los intereses de los indios y de los mexicanos. Eso fue, y sigue siendo, mi opinión. Tampoco me gustaban las actitudes racistas de muchos de los americanos. No me gustaba tampoco la arrogancia de muchos americanos que presumían que tenían el destino manifiesto de reinar soberanamente por todo norteamérica desde el Mar Atlántico hasta el Pacífico, desde el Polo Norte hasta el istmo de Panamá para cumplir sus "fronteras naturales," como ellos decían, en el planeta. Ahora, díganme Uds., ¿cuales son "las fronteras naturales" de un globo?

(Se sienta en la silla.) Ya para el año 1846, yo sabía que México no podría mantener su poder en las provincias norteñas. ¿Qué puedo decir? Yo era patriota mexicano. Tam-

bién conocía las flaquezas políticas, militares, y económicas de mi país predilecto. Sabía que había sido gran equívoco cuando México abrió su frontera al comercio libre con Estados Unidos. Con el abrir de la ruta de Santa Fe, ya sabía que mi país había convidado al águila rapaz norteña a cenar con el recién nacido cordero de la libertad al sur del Río Arkansas. Los yanquis venían a centenares y luego por los miles por ese sendero. Sí, sí, es cierto que traían consigo sus productos comerciales tan tentadoras, esas mercancías fabricadas tan superiores a las que podíamos obtener de México. ¡Y tan obtenibles en tanta abundancia! ¿Y México? Muchos años después de mi época un general mexicano, Porfirio Díaz, si me acuerdo bien, ese gran traidor del liberalismo mexicano, dijo algo que se pudiera aplicar a toda la historia mexicana desde comienzos de la nación:—Pobre México, tan lejos de Dios y tan cerca de los Estados Unidos.—La riqueza de Estados Unidos era demasiado tentadora para muchos de nuestros mexicanos que no podían resistir. Algunos de mi propia familia se hicieron flecheros en ese camino de Santa Fe. Cada vez más, los de mi familia miraban hacia "St. Louis" de Estados Unidos y hacia el este en vez de mirar hacia el sur, hacia la Ciudad de México. Hasta el gobernador Manuel Armijo se enredó con los negocios de la ruta de Santa Fe hasta tal punto que, aunque fuera mexicano hasta el tuétano, ganaba su dinero en Estados Unidos.

Yo sabía que la época cambiaba, que los cambios eran inevitables. En el año 1846, tenía yo 53 años de edad. Había vivido más tiempo que se esperaba. Había vivido suficiente para ver que esos dos jugadores que siempre cabalgan por los senderos obscuros y tenebrosos del destino, esos dos jugadores, el tiempo y la suerte, destruían lo que quedaba del imperio español en el nuevo mundo. Había vivido demasiado ya para ver que el tiempo y la suerte me habían llevado a mi mujer y a mi hija. Y ahora en la vejez, estaba yo viendo que el tiempo y la suerte traían a estos americanos en números siempre crescientes a Nuevo México. Por cierto, pensaba yo, el tiempo y la suerte ya han acabado conmigo porque ya estoy viejo y no aguanto más. Hay un remolino de viento que se acumula en el norte y ya está para descender sobre nosotros y no puedo hacer nada más que cuidar de mi rebaño con la poca fuerza que me queda. Cada momento de mi vida se ha ido al reino de los sueños y aún desde el reino del porvenir vienen nuevos sueños. Al fin y al cabo, estos sueños son sueños, y los sueños sueños son. ¿Por qué nos agitan tanto? Ya la vida me cansaba mucho.

12

(*De repente el humor cambia. El Padre Martínez encuentra la fuerza muy dentro de su ser para un renacimiento de su energía. Se pone de pie y está muy animado.*)

Pero quizás, como saben Uds., no hay nada como un buen discurso emocionante para animar hasta a los viejos. Pues al momento de recibir noticias de la entrada de las tropas norteamericanas y del discursito del comandante, pues me animé. A mí no me pescaron dormido los americanos. Me trajeron noticias de que los soldados vestidos de azul habían salido del fuerte de Bent en el Río Arkansas y que habían bajado por el paso de Ratón. Marchaban rumbo a Santa Fe, por supuesto, y al fin llegarían al Océano Pacífico. Y me contaron lo que dijo aquel comandante, el coronel Stephen Watts Kearny, cuando entró a Las Vegas, esa ciudad donde hay unas vegas formadas por un río que dividen los llanos de las montañas que se llaman la sangre de Cristo. El coronel Kearny se puso de pie en el techo de una casa allí que daba a la plaza vieja y se dirigió a los nuevos ciudadanos norteamericanos de los cuales muy pocos sabían ni una jota del inglés. El coronel Kearny les dijo, según me informaron:—No tomaré posesión ni de una cebolla suya, ni de un chile que les pertenezca sin obtener primero su permiso.— Y luego el buen coronel añadio de prisa:—El que se alza en rebelión contra mi gobierno, a ése lo voy a ahorcar inmediatamente. Así es que no hay que hablar demasiado de las misericordias tan tiernas de nuestros conquistadores.

(En esta escena se dirige al público a veces y otras veces se dirige a los espectros de Willa Cather y del obispo Lamy. El padre anda alrededor de la silla como si fuera el foco central de su proceso.)

¿Pues que se podía hacer? Claro que había entre nosotros los que nos aconsejaban la resistencia militar. *(Mira hacia atrás, hacia el fondo y a la derecha de la escena.)* ¿Qué hubiera hecho Ud., señora Cather? ¿Ud. que tenía esas preocupaciones por la honra y las cosas finas de la vida? ¿Qué de-

biera haber hecho yo como ciudadano leal mexicano? Ah,
¿Y Ud. señor obispo? Era el momento de la gloria de la gran
nación liberal protestante norteamericana. ¿Qué hubiera
hecho su Excelencia? Dada la opinión tan negativa que Ud.
tenía de los nuevomexicanos, ¿piensa Ud. que la entrada de
Estados Unidos era preferible a la soberanía mexicana? ¿A
pesar de que las iglesias protestantes eran tan fuertes en la
nación norteamericana?

(*Se dirige al público.*) Sí, es cierto que hubo los que aconsejaban la resistencia militar. Y entiéndanme muy a las
claras. Si hubiera pensado que la resistencia militar pudiera
haber salvado las provincias norteñas mexicanas de esta invasión injustificada, yo hubiera personalmente encabezado
nuestras tropas para combatir porque así era nuestra tradición desde los tiempos antiguos en España. Hubo muchas
veces en España cuando los curas llevaban espadas debajo
de las sotanas para mejor salir más pronto al campo de ba-
talla contra los moros. Aunque siempre fui hombre de paz,
no obstante me sentía muy cómodo con la idea del cura
guerrero.

Yo sabía, sin embargo, que aquí en Nuevo México no
teníamos el poder militar para resistir los ataques tan fre-
cuentes de los navajoes, los apaches, y los comanches.
Cómo íbamos a resistir el avance de un ejército bien orga-
nizado, y bien abastecido con comida y provisiones de toda
clase? Porque yo sabía que además de esos soldados vestidos de azul, había miles y miles más de soldados norteamericanos que se podían mandar para aplastar la resistencia
militar.

Así pues, aconsejé otro tipo de resistencia. Animé a mi

gente a que fuera fiel a su religión, a su cultura, y a su idioma. Me quedé con mi pueblo durante ese tiempo tenebroso. Jamás pensé aceptar la oferta del tratado de Guadalupe Hidalgo y salir de Nuevo México para vivir en lo que quedaba de México más allá de la nueva frontera. Me quedé com mi pueblo en un tiempo tenebroso. Les exhorté que aprendieran las maneras y las manías de los americanos, y también que se mantuvieran fiel a lo que era lo suyo para mejor aguantar y sobrevivir hasta que llegara una época mejor. El tiempo y la suerte ya jugaban con mi pueblo y me quedé con la gente como cura de Taos.

13

Ya por cierto, pensé yo, el tiempo y la suerte no me harán más travesuras. ¿Verdad que pensamos así cuando hemos sufrido demasiado? ¿Y verdad que casi siempre nos equivocamos? Porque a esos dos jugadores, el tiempo y la suerte, les gusta sacarnos las cartas de abajo. Siempre nos sacan cartas de abajo.

Claro que había nuevomexicanos que no les gustaba escuchar la voz de la razón. Había impetuosos en el pueblo. Se fomentaban dificultades. Donde siempre se fomentan en Nuevo México. En Taos. Ocurrió una conspiración contra los americanos en diciembre de 1846, pero la descubrieron a tiempo. Luego, dentro de pocas semanas, en el mes de enero de 1847, ocurrió una tragedia. Un gentío de Taos, unos rebeldes, atacaron y mataron al gobernador Bent, el primer gobernador territorial designado por los americanos. Los rebeldes también mataron a Narciso Beaubien y a Vigil, el alguacil. Pues yo daba un paseo a la iglesia para celebrar la misa cuando los rebeldes vinieron hacia mí calle abajo. Cuando descubrí lo que había ocurrido, censuré al gentío y les exhorté que se dejaran de estas locuras. Oculté cuantas familias pude en mi propia casa para prevenir que los rebeldes les hicieran daño. El tal "levantamiento de Taos," como se llamó este acontecimiento, acabó en desastre para los rebeldes. Hubo muchos muertos. Ahorcaron a los jefes de la sublevación. Fue la obra del comandante de los americanos, el coronel Sterling Price. *(Se dirige hacia la señora Cather.)* Ah, ahora me recuerdo, señora Cather, de lo que Ud. me echó en cara en esa su novela. Palabras que me acusaban de ser responsable por la sublevación de Taos. ¿Qué extraño, verdad, que me eligieron representante a la Asamblea Territorial *después* de la sublevación en Taos? ¿Qué piensa Ud. de eso, señora Cather? ¿Cree Ud. que sus compatriotas, los americanos eran tan inocentes, tan fáciles de engañar que hubieran elegido como Presidente de la Asamblea Territorial a un hombre que había encabezado un levantamiento militar contra su poder? *(Se dirige al público.)* Ah, ¡qué mujer!

Y así acabó ese episodio trágico. La época mexicana se retiró hacia el mundo de los sueños, como antes lo había hecho la época española. Y nosotros, los nuevomexicanos, pues nos impusimos a aguantar, a sobrevivir, y a tratar de entender nuestros nuevos conquistadores. Eso era difícil porque teníamos que luchar con el idioma nuevo, con las escuelas nuevas, con las leyes nuevas, las reglas comerciales nuevas, y en un ambiente en que los americanos que hablaban el inglés dominaban todas las instituciones políticas, sociales, y económicas.

14

Era bastante difícil sin tener que ajustarse a un nuevo obispo. Nosotros, los curas nuevomexicanos, pues estábamos muy contentos bajo la jurisdicción de Durango. Después del cambio de gobierno y la llegada al poder de los americanos, había rumores de vez en cuando de que se haría una nueva diócesis aquí en Nuevo México pero no sabíamos nada de cómo la Santa Madre Iglesia administraba su reinado espiritual dentro de esta nación de habla inglesa. La verdad es que corría la voz que si se iba a hacer un nuevo obispado entonces sería yo quien se nombraría como obispo. Al fin y al cabo había yo educado a muchos de los jóvenes curas y ellos abogaban por mi causa. Pero yo no tenía nada que ver con esto. No buscaba yo honores. La idea ni se me había ocurrido. Pero sí había rumores por ese lado. Claro, si me hubieran designado, pues, eso era lo lógico. Pero como ya he dicho, jamás busqué tales honores. Ni se me había ocurrido. Entonces pueden imaginarse la sorpresa de nuestros curas mexicanos cuando supimos que nos llegaba un nuevo obispo, un tal padre que se llamaba don Juan Lamy, francés, que venía a Santa Fe. El obispo Jean Baptiste Lamy. Cura francés que no hablaba muy bien ni el inglés ni el español.

¿Pues que se podía hacer? Traté de ver que el nuevo obispo se sintiera cómodo en su casa. *(Se dirige al espectro del obispo.)* ¿Verdad, ilustrísimo señor obispo, don Juan Lamy? No pude asistir a su llegada en Santa Fe durante el mes de agosto de 1851, ¿pero recuerda Ud. como nos hicimos muy buenos amigos cuando llegó Ud. a Taos a principios del año siguiente, en el mes de marzo? ¿Recuerde, señor, las buenas charlas que tuvimos cerca del derecho canónico y la teología? Todavía quisiera hablar con Ud. sobre estos temas. Ud. recuerde cuánto le gustaba mi seminario y quería a los jóvenes que yo educaba para que se hicieran curas. Tenía yo entonces la ilusión que podríamos ser buenos amigos, pero Ud. no lo permitió, ¿verdad, ilustrísimo señor obispo? Pronto se cansó Ud. del interés que yo tenía en el derecho canónico y permitió que su amiguito, sí ese sutil cura, el Señor Cura Machebeuf, le desviara a Ud. del sendero de la paz y la cooperación con los curas nuevomexicanos.

(Mirando alternativamente hacia el público, al obispo, y a Willa Cather, el Padre Martínez está muy consciente de los dos públicos.)

¡Machebeuf! Ese cura no sabía respetar el secreto de la confesión. ¡Machebeuf! ¡Enredador! Llevaba chismes de los curas. Ah, pero Ud., señor, le escuchaba, ¿verdad, mi ilustrísimo señor? ¿Y Ud., señora Cather, ya que era novelista, no podía ver más en lo hondo de las cosas? No, Ud. vió nomás la amistad entre el obispo y el padre Machebeuf. ¿Cómo le llamaba Ud. al padre Machebeuf en su novela? ¡Ah, sí, el padre Vaillant! ¡Nombre de categoría! Ud.

no se dio cuenta, claro, de que esas amistades pudieran crear un nido de víboras—mentiras de mí mismo, mentiras de los curas nuevomexicanos, y crear también una cresciente desilusión por parte del clero de habla español con el primer obispo en Nuevo México bajo las nuevas leyes.

Mas todavía nos quedaba tiempo al obispo y a mí para buscar salida de nuestra falta de acuerdo. Si el ambiente no hubiera estado tan cargado de chisme, tal vez todo hubiera terminado de una manera distinta. Ya para el año 1856, andaba yo en los sesenta y tres años de edad. Sabía bien que se me acababa la vida. De ninguna manera quería yo dejar esta vida sin resolver este ambiente de enredos. Me esforcé de nuevo en ser buen amigo del obispo. Sí, es verdad que protesté el abuso de la confesión del padre Machebeuf, pero esa oposición al padre Machebeuf llevaba implícita la lealtad al obispo. *(Se dirige al espectro del obispo.)* Es cierto que me equivoqué del poder de la amistad entre los dos franceses, ¿verdad, ilustrísimo señor mío? Oh, Uds. eran tan íntimos amigos. Jamás pensé que la crítica que hice del Señor Cura Machebeuf por razón de mi lealtad a su ilustrísimo señor y a la iglesia, pudiera amargar tanto nuestra amistad antigua. Ud. demostró muy a las claras a quien apoyaba. Eso no se le quito a su ilustrísimo señor.

(Dirigiéndose hacia el público.) Escribí una carta al obispo quejándome de mis enfermedades y de la vejez y le ofrecí renunciar mi puesto de cura de Taos si él, el obispo, me permitía preparar a un joven cura como mi sucesor. Esta súplica no parecía fuera de razón, tomando en consideración la edad avanzada mía y también el amplio conocimiento que yo tenía de Nuevo México. El obispo, sin em-

bargo, hizo algo que me afrentó y me entristeció. Prefirió el obispo interpretar mi carta como una renuncia. Hizo la vista gorda a la condición mía. Y en vez de mandarme un joven cura que yo pudiera preparar como sucesor, me mandó ese español tan áspero, el padre Dámaso Taladrid. El Señor Cura Taladrid prosiguió a hacerme la vida muy pesada. Me negó los acólitos para asistirme en la celebración de la misa.

Me tocó en lo vivo cuando negó permitirme celebrar las bodas de mi sobrina. Celebré la misa de todos modos, claro, y por fin el obispo me quitó al Señor Cura Taladrid de encima y de la parroquia. *(Se dirige al espectro del obispo)* Y aún le doy las gracias por eso, mi ilustrísimo señor obispo. *(Dirigiéndose al público.)* Pero ya el chisme, la soberbia terca, y la malicia habían hecho mucho daño.

15

Como pueden ver Uds., había ciertos problemas que apartaban el clero nuevomexicano del obispo, incluso mi propia persona, desde luego. Existía, por ejemplo, ese penoso problema de la catedral. Cuando el obispo Lamy llegó a Santa Fe, esperaba yo que con el tiempo vendría él a apreciar y admirar la catedral de San Francisco. La vieja catedral de adobe. El obispo le dio una mirada y le llamó un "palacio de soquete." No le gustaba la construcción de adobe. Quiso construir la nueva catedral siguiendo la estética románica, una catedral de piedra dura y fría, a la cual estaba acostumbrado en Lempdes, que queda en la parte sur de Francia. El problema tenía que ver con el dinero y cómo adquirirlo. Con la separación americana del estado y la iglesia, no había ni esperanza allí de financiar el proyecto de construcción. En fin, el obispo tenía que sacar el dinero de donde siempre lo han sacado en Nuevo México, de los pobres que menos pueden pagar. Entonces el obispo promulgó su famoso Circular al Clero de 1854, que impuso un nuevo diezmo bajo pena de excomunicación para los que no cumplieran con el diezmo. Se nos prohibía a nosotros, los curas, bautizar a los niños sin primero imponer el nuevo diezmo. Se nos prohibía casar a los jóvenes en la Santa Madre Iglesia sin primero imponer el nuevo diezmo. Se prohibía, además, a los curas enterrar a los difuntos en el camposanto sin recoger primero el nuevo diezmo. Estudié ese circular con mucho cuidado. Me di cuenta de que el obispo simplemente no entendía el sistema de baratas que tenía la sociedad nuevomexicana. Pues entonces no le puse atención al circular. Y seguí bautizando a los niños, casando a los jóvenes, y enterrando a los muertos en el camposanto. Y como siempre me mantuve recogiendo huevos y gallinas, pequeñas bolsas de frijoles y maíz, carne de cabra, pieles de venado, y aceptando otras tales cosas en vez de dinero porque aquí en Nuevo México había muy poco dinero. Y yo esperaba que tarde o temprano el obispo vería que se había equivocado con su circular y que lo quitaría.

Y había entonces también el asunto del arte bello y venerado de nuestros santeros, nuestros talladores que hacían bultos, o sea santos tallados en redondo, y retablos, o tallados llanos para decorar las iglesias. Nuestros santeros tenían muy pocos modelos para su obra de mano. De vez en cuando llegaban de Europa o de México dibujos en una Biblia, o dibujos de santos, o un cuadro raro de tema religioso. Pero para la mayor parte de nuestros santeros tenían que fiarse de su fe y de su imaginación para tallar imágenes para las iglesias. Los primeros santeros trabajaban dentro de una tradición que consideraba su obra como obra venerable de hombres venerables. Y así su obra quedó anónima porque no ponían sus nombres en obra que se dedicaba a Dios y no a sí mismos como artistas. Es decir, no se creían artistas sino humildes servidores de Dios. Pues al obispo Lamy no le gustaban nada nada los tallados de imágenes de santos. El los consideraba como obra del diablo, santos feos y sangrientos, y trató de destruir cuantos santos que pudo. El obispo casi consiguió la destrucción total del arte del santero nuevomexicano. Por supuesto suplantó a los santos destruídos. Los suplantó con litografías baratas que llegaban por la ruta de Santa Fe y después, según me han contado, los suplantó con estatuas de yeso blanco, esas estatuas macizas y feas a las cuales un cínico les atribuyó la calidad de "arte de bata de baño."

Pero lo que causaba más problemas era el asunto de la Santa Hermandad de Nuestro Padre Jesús Nazareno, mejor conocido a Uds., tal vez, como los penitentes, así llamados por razón de sus actos de mortificación porque se flagelaban durante la Semana Santa. Aquí en Nuevo México, donde teníamos muy pocos curas, la Santa Hermandad hacía buenas obras para el pueblo y ayudaba a conservar el ambiente religioso en los pueblos desparramados por dondequiera. El último padre franciscano en la provincia me dio permiso de ser el consejero espiritual de la tercera orden de San Francisco, y de esa manera ayudé a mis hermanos lo mejor que pude para organizar sus moradas donde se juntaban para sus ceremonias religiosas, porque según mi opinión, se asemejaban mucho a la tercera orden. El obispo Lamy, con sus recuerdos aún vivos y negativos de la revolución francesa, consideraba a los penitentes como un peligro para su propia autoridad, algo como un estado subversivo dentro del estado y prosiguió a suprimir a las hermandades. Pues ¿qué podía hacer yo? Era su consejero espiritual de los hermanos. Proseguí en asistirles a mantener fuerte su organización para que pudieran mejor tratar con las nuevas condiciones creadas por los Estados Unidos al subir al poder en este territorio.

A pesar de mis esfuerzos de conservar la amistad del obispo, parecía que nuestras diferencias, y tal vez también nuestras comunicaciones siempre tan difíciles, se alimentaban a sí mismos y todo se fue de mal en peor. De todos modos, el obispo mandó su amigo desagradable, el Señor Cura Machebeuf, a Taos para "azotar a los gatos," como él solía decir. Vino a Taos, entonces, para leer la carta de excomunicación. Le supliqué a mi gente que escucharan respetuosamente al Señor Cura Machebeuf y así los fieles se quedaron sentados en silencio mientras que él fulminaba contra mi persona. Algunos de los americanos, invasores de tierras y oportunistas que me odiaban, hombres como Kit Carson, Carlos Beaubien, y Ceran St. Vrain trataron de hacer correr chismes de que habría violencia pero siempre fui hombre de paz. A veces yo era muy cabezudo, sí, pero en lo mero principal yo era hombre de paz.

16

¿Y qué pensaba yo de la excomunicación? No me gustaba.
Y no lo creía. El obispo había ignorado los procedimientos
del derecho canónico. Pues, entre más pensaba en la excomunicación, más me daba cuenta de que no valía el papel
en que se había escrito. Sabía que como yo era abogado
eclesiástico, algo que apenas he mencionado, podía haber
aplastado tal excomunicación si hubiera sido más joven y
más fuerte para hacer el largo y penoso viaje a Roma. El
obispo sabía que no era cierto que saldría con la suya en
Roma. *(Dirigiéndose al obispo.)* ¿No es así, mi ilustrísimo señor? *(Dirigiéndose de nuevo al público.)* Se daba cuenta de que
yo sabía esto. Y me dejó en paz. Fingió que yo ya no existía.
Pero muy prudentemente el obispo no trató de sacarme de
mi iglesia en Taos. Pues no hice caso a la excomunicación.
Y seguí como siempre aceptando cabritos y gallinas y ristras de chile como pago para los servicios religiosos que yo
oficiaba. Y seguí suministrando a los menesteres de mis
fieles nuevomexicanos.

(Dirigiéndose al obispo.) Quizás pensaba Ud. que no viviría
yo mucho tiempo después de la excomunicación, ¿verdad?
Pues le engañé a Ud. *(Se dirige al público.)* Y yo mismo me
engañé. Parecía que a lo menos por una temporada tenía
más energía. Hasta me interesaba la política otra vez. Mas
por la mayor parte, suministré a los menesteres de mi
pueblo. No era tan fácil para un anciano como quizás Uds.
creen.

Una noche oí gritos y exclamaciones. Una mujer que lloraba en pena. Se me acercaron los ruidos hasta que alguien dio golpes fuertes en la puerta que daba a la calle. Y luego se quebró la puerta. Era Juan Sánchez y su mujer, María. El parecía disparatado y tenía los ojos grandes y locos. Había puesto su faja en el cuello de su mujer y ella tenía un miedo escalofriante. Era ella la que había dado razguñazos y golpes fuertes a la puerta y ahora, medio muerta del terror y de la falta de respiración por razón de la faja que le sofocaba, cayó de rodillas (el Padre Martínez demuestra) y gritó —¡Padre, socorro, sálveme!—

—¿Qué pasa aquí?, les pregunté. —¡Y quítale esa faja!—

—¡Andaba de puta!— Eso es lo que Juan Sánchez me dijo.

—¿Y ahora quieres ser el verdugo?— le grité.

—¡Quítale esa faja!— también le grité otra vez. Muy despacio aflojó la faja y la dejó caer. Entonces comenzó a llorar.

—Y tú,— le dije a ella, —¿qué andabas de puta?—

—Sí, padre. Es verdad. Lo siento mucho— ella dijo. Y comenzó a temblar y llorar.

Pues, con toda esta lloradera, tenía yo ganas de llorar también. Y los agarré a los dos y les di una sacudida fuerte. Me dirigí entonces a Juan Sánchez y le dije —¿qué no te vi ayer cayéndote al salir de la cantina y también tomando vino a grandes tragos?—

—Sí, padre— dijo.

—Pues esa botella es tu puta,— lo regañé. —Si no perdieras tanto tiempo con tu puta botella quizás pudieras estar más tiempo con tu mujer.—

—Y tú— le dije a María, —¿qué diablos hacías de vagamunda puta?—

—No sé, padre— ella dijo. Y lloró a rienda suelta.

¿Pues que podía hacer? Estaba casi para regañarla más fuerte aún cuando me recordé del cuento de Jesús y la mujer que la pescaron en el adulterio. Los fariseos le llevaron a Jesús una mujer adúltera y él rehusó condenarla. Recogió unas piedras y luego dijo: —El que esté sin pecado entre Uds., que le tira la primera piedra.— Uno a uno los fariseos se apartaron de Jesús y de la pobre mujer.

No podía yo tirar la primera piedra. Recordé las muchas veces que me sentí defraudado por la vida. Recordé cuando perdí a mi esposa linda y joven en el momento del parto hacía tantos años. Y no podía tirar la primera piedra. Recordé la muerte repentina de mi hija. Yo no podía tirar la primera piedra. Recordé lo vacío que me sentí muy dentro de mi ser cuando hubo muertos en la guerra de los chimayosos. Y no podía tirar la primera piedra. Recordé la nostalgia que sentí por todo un mundo que se desaparecía cuando me informaron de la invasión de Estados Unidos. Y no podía tirar la primera piedra. Recordé la llegada del nuevo obispo a Santa Fe y cómo todas mis esperanzas de una carrera eclesiástica se volvieron humo. Y no podía yo tirar la primera piedra. Ahora sufrían estos dos que estaban de pie aquí. Dos pecadores como yo era pecador, y los tres sufriendo con el dolor inevitable del vivir. Y yo no podía tirar la primera piedra. Los abracé a los dos. Les conté el cuento de Jesús y de la mujer esa. Ah, entonces vi cara a cara a Juan Sánchez porque yo sabía bien que él se había acostado no únicamente con su mujer o con una botella de vino. Bajó la vista y no dijo nada. Y le dije a María que sería más feliz si se pasara menos tiempo en la cantina y se

dedicara más a leer, a aprender, y a auydarme en mi vejez
para educar a sus hijos. Me dieron las gracias y se fueron
en silencio.

¿Tuvieron problemas después? No sé por cierto pero
probablemente sí. Eso es muy humano, ¿verdad? Espero
que su porvenir les haya traído los sueños que tenían y que
no haya habido mucho de los malos sueños, las pesadillas.
Después de que se fueron me senté por largo rato en la sala
de mi casa. De repente sentí el peso de la vejez y me sentía
fatigado. Demasiada emoción para un cura viejo. Había
visto yo demasiado sufrir en mi vida.

Y sabía también que el obispo sufría. El no podría gozar
más que yo del estado de relaciones entre nosotros. Pero él
era más joven y yo sabía que el tiempo y la suerte le qui-
tarían muy pronto el peso que cargaba conmigo. Recordé
que si mi hija hubiera vivido, hubiera tenido un año menos
que el joven obispo francés. Mas el tiempo y la suerte nos
traen a todos a una condición donde el tiempo humano y la
suerte humana dejan de existir. Decimos que en cien años
todos seremos calvos.

17

Al día siguiente, recogí todos mis papeles y preparé mi último testamento. Repartí las pocas posesiones que tenía
entre mis numerosos parientes. No se me olvidaron los
huérfanos a quienes había dado el nombre de Martínez. *(Se
dirige al espectro de Willa Cather.)* Estos eran mis "hijos," se-

ñora Cather. Lástima que Ud. no escribió nada de ellos. Comprendo, por supuesto, qu la novela tiene su propia verdad. Es igual con la historia, señora Cather. Si Ud. tan siquiera hubiera tenido un poco más de compasión conmigo. Por otra parte, quizás Ud. sufre como el buen obispo. Si Ud. hubiera vivido unas decenas de años antes, quizás nos hubiéramos conocido y tal vez hubiera tenido una opinión distinta de mí. Al fin y al cabo, todos somos hijos, huérfanos en el exilio de este mundo, de este sueño terrestre donde nos preparamos para el mejor sueño del porvenir que nos espera más allá.

(Dirigiéndose al público.) Hasta en este sueño que vivimos hay gente que tiene cariño para los huérfanos. Pues por esta razón dejé algunas cosas para la señora doña Teodora. Como recompensa por sus muchos años de servicio a la iglesia. Y también como me sirvió a mí . . . ah, pero no quiero dar lugar al escándalo. No, no, no quiero entrar en esto en todos los detalles. Podrá haber otra Willa Cather oculta allá en lo oscuro. Permítanme decir que doña Teodora era mujer buena y amable y yo la recompensé por sus méritos.

Al dar cuenta de mis posesiones materiales, escogí mi propio epitafio. Es una cita que encontré en el Antiguo Testamento, en el libro de Eclesiastés, capítulo nueve, verso once:

> Volví
> Y vi bajo el sol
> Que la carrera no es de los ligeros
> Ni la batalla de los fuertes . . .

Mas el tiempo y la suerte
Les ocurre a todos.

El tiempo y la suerte, esos dos jugadores que me habían quitado tanto. Mas también me habían dado la oportunidad de reflejar en mis propios tiempos y en mi vida. Me enseñaron a ser bastante humilde para ver que nunca dominamos tanto nuestro destino como quisiéramos pensar. Ni yo. Ni tú. Tampoco ni la señora Cather ni el obispo.

Lo único que podemos hacer es trabajar y gozar de la vida juntos. Y muchas veces tenemos que llorar. Porque si el tiempo y la suerte me han enseñado a lo menos algo, es que tenemos que tratar de cicatrizar las heridas que causamos el uno al otro. Quizás allí está la clave a este misterio tragicómico cósmico en el cual vagamos. Sí, vagamos en este viaje celestial y tenemos oportunidad de cicatrizar nuestras heridas, de ayudarnos el uno al otro. Tal vez el tiempo y la esperanza, esos dos jugadores ancianos son los empleados de alguien que conoce todas las posibilidades. *(Se ríe)* Tal vez Dios sí juega a los dados.

Ah, pero ya empiezo a tener algo de sacerdote. Y ya debiera alejarme. Algún día, en algún lugar, pronto, en este viaje celestial, espero encontrar al obispo. *(Mira hacia el fondo del teatro.)* Pudiera estar oculto por aquí cerca. El y yo no tenemos pleitos sobre el dogma y la teología de la iglesia. Pero quisiera discutir ciertos aspectos del derecho canónico con él. Hay algunos temas allí de los cuales él y yo tenemos que buscar un acuerdo. Y algún día muy pronto confío en que me encuentre con la señora Cather. Quisiera discutir con ella la teoría de la ficción en comparación con

la de la historia. *(Mira otra vez al fondo de la escena.)* Estará
por allá escribiendo algo. Tengo ansias de hablar con ella.

Y ahora, mis hijos, debiera alejarme, porque el viaje es
largo y apenas lo he comenzado. Espero que nos encontre-
mos muy pronto otra vez y que podamos continuar nuestras
discusiones de estos asuntos tan graves. Hay que recordar
que debemos viajar con poco equipaje. Ahora viajo con
menos equipaje que una sombra, con el poco peso de los
rasgos de mi vida que dejo sus mentes, en sus recuerdos,
en sus sueños. Adiós.

FIN.